English for academic study:

Reading and Writing

Source Book

John Slaght, Paddy Harben
and Anne Pallant

D1357605

EDUCATION

University of
Reading

Credits

Published by
Garnet Publishing Ltd.
8 Southern Court
South Street
Reading RG1 4QS, UK

This edition first published 2006

ISBN-10: 1 85964 840 1
ISBN-13: 978 1 85964 840 7

British Cataloguing-in-Publication Data
A catalogue record for this book is available from
the British Library.

Production
Project manager: Richard Peacock
Project consultant: Rod Webb
Editorial team: Lucy Thompson, Angela Langridge,
                       Francesca Pinagli
Design: Mike Hinks
Illustration: Mike Hinks, Doug Nash
Photography: Corbis: Robert Essel NYC,
                       Jeremy Horner, Caroline Penn,
                       Michael Prince, Franco Vogt,
                       Roger Wilmshurst; Mike Hinks;
                       The United Nations.

Printed and bound
in Lebanon by International Press

The authors and publishers wish to acknowledge the
following use of material:

'Economics focus: On the move' © The Economist
Newspaper Limited, London (May 12th, 2001).

'Does Class Size Matter?' reprinted with permission.
Copyright © 2001 by *Scientific American*, Inc.
All rights reserved.

Atkinson, R.L. *et al.*, *Hilgard's Introduction to Psychology*,
13th edition (1999). © 1996. Reprinted with permission
of Wadsworth, a division of Thomson Learning:
www.thomsonrights.com. Fax 800 730-2215

Middleton, N., 'Acid rain in Norway' in *Geography
Review*, Vol. 11, No. 4 (1998). Reprinted with
permission © Philip Allan Updates.

Everett, M., 'Impact – Skylarks in decline' in *Biological
Sciences Review*, Vol. 10, No. 2 (1997). Reprinted with
permission © Philip Allan Updates.

'Ring in the new' © The Economist Newspaper Limited,
London (October 7th, 1999)

'Beyond the bubble' © The Economist Newspaper
Limited, London (October 9th, 2003)

'Statistics Without Tears: A Primer for Non-Mathematicians'
by Derek Rowntree (Penguin Books, 1982). Copyright ©
Derek Rowntree, 1982. Pages 14–21 reproduced by
permission of Penguin Books Ltd.

'Common Questions about Climate Change'
(pages 4–12), reprinted with permission © United
Nations Environment Programme and World
Meteorological Organization.

'The Global Village: Challenges for a Shrinking
Planet', reprinted with permission from *The Global
Village: Challenges for a Shrinking Planet* (*Understanding
Global Issues 98/7*).

'The New Linguistic Order' in *Foreign Policy*, Winter
1998–99 (pages 26–39), Joshua A. Fishman.

Contents

Text i–1: Economics focus: On the move

FINANCE AND ECONOMICS   The Economist, May 12th, 2001

Economics focus: On the move

Economic analysis sheds light on the history of immigration and on its future

During the spread of globalisation in the three centuries leading up to the first world war, the migration of workers was consistently one of the biggest causes of economic change. Since 1945, the world has experienced a new era of globalisation which is much quicker, and the international movement of labour is proving once again to be of the greatest significance. That is so despite the efforts of governments in richer countries to restrict migration, and despite basic changes in its economic nature. As a new study* by Barry Chiswick of the University of Illinois at Chicago and Timothy Hatton of the University of Essex makes plain, it is economic factors that have been the most important throughout the history of migration.

For many years after the discovery of America, the movement of free migrants from Europe was steady but quite small: transport costs were high, conditions harsh and the dangers of migration great. In 1650, a free migrant's passage to North America cost nearly half a year's wages for a farm labourer in southern England. Indentured work developed as a way around this. This meant that the workers were forced to work for their bosses for a period of time without pay. However, direct slavery dominated until the slave trade was stopped in the first half of the 19th century. By around 1800, North America and the Caribbean Islands had received some 8m immigrants. Of these, about 7m were African slaves.

The first era of mass voluntary migration was between 1850 and 1913. Over 1m people a year were attracted to the new world by the turn of the 20th century. Growing prosperity, falling transport costs relative to wages and lower risk all

Economic analysis sheds light on the history of immigration and on its future

pushed in the same direction.

Between 1914 and 1945, war, global depression and government policy helped to reduce migration dramatically. During some years in the 1930s, people returning to Europe from the United States, even though comparatively few, actually outnumbered immigrants going the other way – a rare case for America of net emigration.

After the second world war the economics of migration reasserted itself. The cost of travel fell steeply. But now the pattern changed. Before long Europe declined as a source of immigration and grew as a destination. Emigration from developing countries expanded rapidly: incomes there rose enough to make emigration feasible, but not enough to make it pointless. Many governments began trying to control immigration. The numbers of legal and illegal immigrants grew nonetheless, as economics had its way

Winners and Losers

Migration, it is safe to assume, is in the interests of (voluntary) migrants: they would not move otherwise. The evidence suggests that it is also very much in the overall interests of the receiving countries. But, as Chiswick and Hatton point out, there are losers in those countries. The increase in the supply of labour presses down the wages of competing workers, at least in the first instance. (Later, as the stock of capital grows in response, that effect may be partially reversed.)

The economic conditions now seem favourable for an enormous further expansion of migration. On the face of it, this will be much like that of a century ago. As before, the main expansionary pressures are rising incomes in the rich countries and rising incomes in the poor ones. (This second point is often neglected: as poor countries get a little less poor, emigration tends to increase, because people acquire the resources to move.) The study emphasises, however, two crucial differences between then and now.

One is that, in the first decade of the 20th century, the receiving countries needed lots of unskilled workers in industry and farming. In the first decade of the 21st century, in contrast, opportunities for unskilled workers who can migrate are decreasing. In America, wages of unskilled workers are falling, in absolute as well as relative terms. The fall is enough to hurt the workers concerned, but not to deter new immigrants. Several studies suggest that immigration has made a definite contribution to this decline.

And the other big difference between now and a century ago? It is that the affected rich-country workers are in a stronger position to complain, and get something done. The most likely result is that a trend that is already well established (either as explicit policy or customary practice) will continue: countries will try to restrict the immigration of unskilled workers, giving preference to workers with skills.

This does help, in one way, quite apart from reducing the skills deficit in rich countries: it eases the downward pressure on wages at the bottom. However, the idea has disadvantages too. It turns away many of the poorest potential migrants, which is hard to justify in humanitarian terms. Also it pushes others from this group into illegal immigration, which exposes them to dangers, makes assimilation more difficult and may even cause a stronger downward pull on the wages of some low-skilled workers in receiving-countries than the legal entry of the same migrants.

On top of all this is the skills drain from the sending countries. Already some of the world's poorest nations lose almost all the doctors they train to jobs in Europe or North America. Financial remittances offset some of that loss, but not all.

Today's migration, much more than the migration of old, causes some insoluble problems. Regard for individual freedom argues for a more liberal immigration regime in the rich countries, and for unskilled migrants as well as skilled ones. With or without such a regime, more migrants are coming. And in either case, the question of compensation for the losers, in rich countries and poor countries alike, will demand some attention.

*Chiswick, Barry R. and Hatton, Timothy J. (August 2002) 'International Migration and the Integration of Labour Markets', ftp://repec.iza.org/RePEc/Discussionpaper/dp559.pdf

THE INFLUENCE OF CLASS SIZE ON ACADEMIC ACHIEVEMENT

Education is a pillar of modern society and the subject of endless, often passionate arguments about how it can best be improved. In the U.S., there is heated 5 debate following revelations that the country's secondary school students perform poorly relative to many Asian and European students. The news coincided with increasing concern over the nation's urban and 10 lower-income suburban schools, too many of which are languishing at achievement levels far below those of middle-class and upper middle-class suburban schools.

Of all the ideas for improving education, 15 few are as simple or attractive as reducing the number of pupils per teacher. With its uncomplicated appeal and lack of a big, powerful group of opponents, class-size reduction has lately developed from a sub-20 ject of primarily academic interest to a key political issue. In the United States, more than 20 states and the federal government have adopted policies aimed at decreasing class sizes, and billions of dollars have been 25 spent or committed in the past few years. The demand for smaller classes is also growing in Canada, Australia, the United Kingdom, and even Japan, whose record of secondary school performance is the envy of 30 most other developed countries.

The most obvious drawback to class-size reduction is the huge cost. It requires more teachers, more classrooms and more classroom equipment and resources. These 35 expenses can dwarf the price of alternative schemes, such as testing teachers or increasing their pay as a means of attracting better candidates. The state of California, for example, has been spending more than 40 $1.5 billion annually over the past several years to reduce class size to 20 or fewer for children in the four to seven-year-old bracket. On the other hand, if smaller classes really do work, the economic benefits could be huge.

45 They would accrue not just from the benefits of a better-educated workforce but also from other sources, such as the avoided medical costs and sick days of a healthier, more informed populace.

50 The surge of interest in smaller classes has spurred fresh analyses of the largest, most conclusive study to date, which took place in Tennessee in the late 1980s. At the same time, new data are flowing from 55 various initiatives, including the California programme and a smaller one in Wisconsin. These results and analyses are finally offering some tentative responses to the questions that researchers must answer before 60 legislators can come up with policies that make educational and economic sense: Do small classes in fact improve school achievement? If they do, at what age-level do they accomplish the greatest good? What kind of 65 students gain the greatest benefit, and most importantly, how great is the benefit?

WHAT ARE THE BENEFITS OF SMALLER CLASS SIZES?

Educators have a multitude of explanations 70 for why smaller class sizes might be expected to improve academic performance, although frequently the ideas are anecdotal. Fewer students in the classroom seem to translate into less noise and disruptive 75 behaviour from students, which not only gives the teacher more time for class work but also more freedom to engage students creatively – by, for example, dividing them into groups for specific projects. In addition, 80 smaller classes make it more likely that the teacher can give greater individual attention to struggling students. Smaller classes also allow teachers to encourage more discussion, assign more writing and closely exam- 85 ine their students' written work. In other words, much of the benefit of reduced class size may depend on whether the teachers adapt their methods to take advantage of

smaller classes. Finally, some analysts 90 believe that the very youngest age group in smaller classes are more likely to develop good study habits, higher self-esteem and possibly other beneficial cognitive traits – which may very well persist for years, even 95 after the students have gone back to more normal-sized classes.

One way investigators have attempted to analyse the effects of class size is by reviewing existing data, such as records kept by the 100 U.S. Department of Education. These show that between 1969 and 1997, the average number of pupils per teacher in American public and private elementary schools fell from 25.1 to 18.3, a decline of greater than 105 27%. In secondary schools, the number also fell, from 19.7 to 14.0. Of concern, however, is the fact that despite these steep drops in pupil-teacher ratios, the improvement in academic performance was negligible. Data 110 from the National Assessment of Educational Progress – a series of tests that is the only United States-wide indicator of student knowledge in reading, mathematics, science and other subjects – show no significant 115 gains. In some specific age and subject categories, such as 17-year-olds and science, performance actually decreased slightly.

WHAT THE RECORD SHOWS

However, these findings do not necessarily 120 mean that class size makes no difference. For a variety of reasons, most researchers, including the writers, pay little attention to these figures (Figure 1). For instance, schools strive for more than just high test 125 scores; they also usually try to keep their dropout rate low. In fact, the dropout rate for students aged 16–24 fell from 15 to 11 per cent over the period. Because dropouts generally come from the low end of the 130 achievement distribution, a reduction in dropout rate could be expected to pull down average test scores in the upper grades.

FIGURE 1: MILESTONE STUDIES IN CLASS SIZE

PROJECT	STATE	STUDENTS PARTICIPATING	APPROX. COST	SMALL CLASS SIZE	KEY FINDINGS
STAR 1985–89	Tennessee	10,000	$12m	13–17	Significant performance benefit of 0.2 standard deviation; larger gains for minority pupils
Class size reduction	California	1.8m	$5 billion	Less than 20	Small performance gain of about 0.05 to 0.1 standard deviation; no greater gains for minorities
SAGE	Wisconsin	64,000	£103m	12–15	Significant performance advantage of 0.2 standard deviation; larger gains for minority pupils

Another reason for discounting those data goes right to the heart of the difficulties 135 in this field of study: it is hard to isolate the effects of class size from the myriad factors that influence student performance. The reality is that in 1995 only 68% of American students came from families with 140 two parents in the home – down from 85% in 1970. The fraction of children who had difficulty speaking English rose from 2.8% in 1970 to 20.2% in 1995. There was some good news: the median level of education 145 among parents increased slightly during that time period, as did the level among teachers, whose average amount of experience also went up.

Basically, demographic shifts make it 150 very difficult to assess the effect of reductions in pupil-teacher ratios. Well-designed experiments attempt to cancel out the influence of those other factors by randomly assigning students and teachers 155 to different class sizes and by including a large sample. Over the past 35 years, hundreds of studies and analyses of existing data have focused on class size. Most found evidence that smaller classes 160 benefit students, particularly at the youngest level, and especially children in danger of becoming underachievers.

Unfortunately, most of these studies were poorly designed. Teacher and student 165 assignments were rarely sufficiently random; a number of studies were simply too brief or too small, and too few had independent evaluation. The notable exception was the Tennessee study. The distinguished 170 Harvard University statistician, Frederick Mosteller, has called it "one of the greatest experiments in education in United States history". The Student-Teacher Achievement Ratio, better known as Project STAR, was a 175 state-sponsored, $12 million demonstration programme (see Figure 1). Students entering kindergarten were randomly assigned to one of three kinds of classes: a small class of 13 to 17 children, a 180 normal-sized class of 22 to 26 children, or a normal-sized class with both a teacher and a full-time teacher's assistant. The students remained in whatever category they had been assigned to until they had 185 reached the third grade, after which they joined a normal classroom in the fourth. To ensure that teaching quality did not differ, teachers were randomly assigned to small and normal-sized classrooms. Few 190 teachers received any special training for working with small classes, and there were no new curricular materials.

A CASE STUDY: SHINING STAR

After the study ended in 1989, researchers conducted dozens of analyses of the data. One of the few points analysts agree on is that the teacher's assistants did not make any differ-
5 ence to academic performance. Researchers disagree about how long students have to be in smaller classes to get a benefit, how big that benefit is, when it becomes noticeable – in other words, the collected findings have
10 yielded no consensus on the issues of real interest to policymakers.

Jeremy Finn of the State University of New York and Charles M. Achilles of Eastern Michigan University found "an array of
15 benefits of small classes" in their review. Finn calculated that students in the small classes outperformed their counterparts in normal-sized classes by a fifth of a standard deviation, and that this sizable jump in achievement
20 generally appeared by the first grade. Best of all, this advantage seemed to persist into upper elementary levels even after students returned to larger classes. In order to appreciate how big a difference there is in terms of a fifth
25 of a standard deviation, it is necessary to compare two pupils first starting school who are as average as it is possible to be statistically. Both are in the 50th percentile, meaning that half of the other pupils perform better than
30 those two and that half perform worse. One student should be placed in a small class, and the other in a normal-sized class. After a year, the pupil in the small class will be in the 58th percentile – in other words, the student will be
35 doing better than nearly 60% of his or her peers – while the other student will still be doing better than only 50%. Finn and Achilles also found that the effect was stronger for ethnic minority students, by a factor of two

40 or three. In other words, black or Hispanic children improved by two-fifths to three-fifths of a standard deviation – a significant finding from a policy point of view, because minorities typically score about one standard deviation
45 below their peers on standard tests.

A few analysts, notably Eric Hanushek of Stanford University's Hoover Institute, criticise STAR and some of the key conclusions reached by its proponents. Hanushek agrees
50 that students can gain an initial benefit from small classes. But, he argues, the STAR data cannot be used to prove that the gains persist for years after a student has returned to normal-sized classes. If a child is still doing
55 well years later, it is hard to know how much of the performance stems from other factors, such as a supportive home. Hanushek also disagrees with an analysis indicating that the benefits of small classes accumulate – that
60 students who stay in such classes for several years widen the performance gap with their peers in large classes year by year. When he studied the four-year gains of STAR students who were in smaller classes from kindergarten
65 until they reached grade three, he did not find the gains to be larger than those logged in kindergarten. He and others have also shown that during the study, too many children migrated from the regular to the small classes,
70 probably because school personnel caved in to parental demands. Hanushek further asserts that STAR had insufficient checks to ensure good randomisation of teacher and student placement in classes. These are good points,
75 but they do not really undermine the findings of STAR of a statistically significant benefit of being in a class of between 13 and 17, rather than 23, students.

The Authors: RONALD G. EHRENBERG, DOMINIC J. BREWER, ADAM GAMORAN and J. DOUGLAS WILLMS collaborated on a paper surveying studies of class size and academic performance for the May 2001 issue of *Psychological Science in the Public Interest*. Ehrenberg is the Irving M. Ives Professor of Industrial and Labour Relations and Economics at Cornell University and the author of Tuition Rising: *Why College Costs So Much* [Harvard University Press, 2000]. Brewer, who specialises in the economics of education, is the director of Rand Education, which analyses programmes and policies on education issues, and is a visiting professor of economics at the University of California, Los Angeles. Gamoran, a former Fulbright scholar, is a professor of sociology and education policy studies at the University of Wisconsin – Madison. Willms is a professor of the Canadian Research Institute for Social Policy at the University of New Brunswick.

Text 1–3: The Asian paradox: Huge classes, high scores

THE ASIAN PARADOX
HUGE CLASSES, HIGH SCORES

BY GLENN ZORPETTE

Study after study ranks schoolchildren in Japan and other developed Asian countries among the best in the world, particularly on standardised tests of 5 mathematics and science. American high school students, meanwhile, have slipped somewhere below those in Greece, Lithuania, Taiwan and Singapore in advanced mathematics 10 and science. However, classes in Asia are large; forty students for one teacher would be normal in most of the region. In contrast, elementary school class sizes in the United States average about 15 24, according to the U.S. Department of Education.

The question is why Asian children do so well in such large classes. In Japan, for example, the discipline is leg-20 endary. Such discipline is not imposed by fearsome teachers, according to Catherine Lewis, an expert on the Japanese educational system and a senior researcher at Mills College. Instead, 25 students are honoured to be chosen to lead lessons, and they take turns calling the class to order, experiencing firsthand what it is like to quieten down an unruly group of students. As a result, teachers 30 manage the class by relying on 'the cumulative general power of self-reflection, rather than by punishing and rewarding,' Lewis explains. Japanese teachers and students also spend much 35 more time together – the usual year is about 40 days longer than in the United States – and more time bonding with one another at school festivals and on field trips and hikes. 'There's an incredibly 40 strong emphasis on class, group and school being meaningful entities for the children,' Lewis says. Japan's prowess in academic achievement is also sustained by something it does not have: ethnic 45 and linguistic diversity. Finally, Asian parents are far less likely than Americans to be divorced and are more likely to be involved in their children's education.

The downside of the Asian system is 50 that the rigid national standards do not do much to foster creativity. At the same time, in Japan some children strive hard to excel partly because they become burdened early on by the fear of failing. 55 Given the deep cultural differences, it is not clear which parts of the Asian formula could work in other countries such as America. However, the Asian experience does demonstrate what can 60 be done when discipline grows from the bottom up. In that kind of environment, elementary school teachers can focus on 'creating happy memories', as one Japanese teacher described her main 65 purpose to Lewis.

Glenn Zorpette is a writer based in New York.

Source: Ehrenberg, D., Brewer, D.J., Gamoran, A. and Willms, D.J., 'Does Class Size Matter?' in *Scientific American* (November 2001).

Interaction between nature and nurture

A The question of whether heredity ("nature") or environment ("nurture") is more important in determining the course of human development has been debated through the centuries. For example, the seventeenth-century British
5 philosopher John Locke rejected the prevailing notion of his day that babies were miniature adults who arrived in the world fully equipped with abilities and knowledge and who simply had to grow in order for these inherited characteristics to appear. On the contrary,
10 Locke believed that the mind of a newborn infant is a "blank slate" (tabula rasa). What gets written on this slate is what the baby experiences – what he or she sees, hears, tastes, smells and feels. According to Locke, all knowledge comes
15 to us through our senses. It is provided by experience; no knowledge or ideas are built in.

B The advent of Charles Darwin's theory of evolution (1859), which emphasises the biological basis of human development, led to a
20 return of the hereditarian viewpoint. With the rise of behaviourism in the twentieth century, however, the environmentalist position once again gained dominance. Behaviourists such as John B. Watson and B.F. Skinner argued that
25 human nature is completely malleable: early training can turn a child into any kind of adult, regardless of his or her heredity. Watson stated the argument in its most extreme form: "Give me a dozen healthy infants, well-formed, and
30 my own specified world to bring them up in, and I'll guarantee to take any one at random and train him to be any type of specialist I might select – doctor, lawyer, artist, merchant-chief, and yes, beggar-man and thief, regardless of his
35 talents, penchants, tendencies, abilities, vocations, and race of his ancestors" (1930, p.104).

C Today most psychologists agree not only that both nature and nurture play important roles but that they interact continuously to guide development.
40 For example, we shall see in Chapter 12 that the development of many personality traits, such as sociability and emotional stability, appear to be influenced about equally by heredity and environment; similarly, we shall see in Chapter
45 15 that psychiatric illnesses can have both genetic and environmental determinants.

D Even development that seems most obviously to be determined by innate biological timetables can be affected by environmental events. At the
50 moment of conception, a remarkable number of personal characteristics are already determined by the genetic structure of the fertilized ovum. Our genes program our growing cells so that we develop into a person rather than a fish or
55 chimpanzee. They decide our sex, the colour of

Early human development

our skin, eyes, and hair and general body size, among other things. These genetic determinants are expressed in development through the process of maturation – innately determined
60 sequences of growth and change that are relatively independent of environmental events.

E For example, the human fetus develops within the mother's body according to a fairly fixed time schedule, and fetal behaviour, such as
65 turning and kicking, also follows an orderly sequence that depends on the stage of growth. However, if the uterine environment is seriously abnormal in some way, maturational processes can be disrupted. For example, if the mother
70 contracts German measles during the first three months of pregnancy (when the fetus's basic organ systems are developing according to the genetically programmed schedule), the infant may be born deaf, blind or brain-damaged,
75 depending on which organ system was in a critical stage of development at the time of infection. Maternal malnutrition, smoking, and consumption of alcohol and drugs are among the other environmental factors that can affect
80 the normal maturation of the fetus.

F Motor development after birth also illustrates the interaction between genetically programmed maturation and environmental influence. Virtually all children go through the same sequence of
85 motor behaviours in the same order: rolling over, sitting without support, standing while holding onto furniture, crawling, and then walking. But children go through the sequence at different rates, and developmental psychologists began
90 very early in the history of the discipline to ask

whether learning and experience play an important role in such differences.

G Although early studies suggested that the answer was no (McGraw, 1935/1975; Dennis & Dennis,
95 1940; Gesell & Thompson, 1929), more recent studies indicate that practice or extra stimulation can accelerate the appearance of motor behaviours to some extent. For example, newborn infants have a stepping reflex; if they are held in
100 an upright position with their feet touching a solid surface, their legs will make stepping movements that are similar to walking. A group of infants who were given stepping practice for a few minutes several times a day during the first two
105 months of life began walking five to seven weeks earlier than babies who had not had this practice (Zelazo, Zelazo & Kolb, 1972).

H The development of speech provides another example of the interaction between genetically
110 determined characteristics and experience. In the course of normal development, all human infants learn to speak, but not until they have attained a certain level of neurological development; no infant less than a year old
115 speaks in sentences. But children reared in an environment in which people talk to them and reward them for making speechlike sounds talk earlier than children who do not receive such attention. For example, children reared in
120 middle-class American homes begin to speak at about one year of age. Children reared in San Marcos, a remote village in Guatemala, have little verbal interaction with adults and do not utter their first words until they are
125 over two years old (Kagan, 1979).

Atkinson, R.L. *et al.*, *Hilgard's Introduction to Psychology*, 13th edition (1999) pp. 70–71. © 1996.

Capacities
of the newborn

A At the end of the nineteenth century, psychologist William James suggested that the newborn child experiences the world as a "buzzing, blooming confusion", an
5 idea that was still prevalent as late as the 1960s. We now know that newborn infants enter the world with all sensory systems functioning and are well prepared to learn about their new environment.

B Because babies cannot explain what they are doing or tell us what they are thinking, developmental psychologists have had to design some very ingenious procedures to study the capacities of young infants. The basic method
15 is to introduce some change in the baby's environment and observe his or her responses. For example, an investigator might present a tone or a flashing light and then see if there is a change in heart rate or if the baby turns its
20 head or sucks more vigorously on a nipple. In some instances, the researcher will present two stimuli at the same time to determine if infants look longer at one than the other. If they do, it indicates that they can tell the stimuli apart and
25 may indicate that they prefer one to the other.

Vision

C Because the visual system is not well developed at birth, newborns have poor visual acuity, their ability to change focus is limited, and they are very
30 nearsighted. An adult with normal vision is said to have 20/20 vision; a nearsighted adult with 20/30 vision is able to see at 20 feet what an adult with normal vision can see at 30 feet. Using this same index, a newborn had 20/660 vision. At six
35 months this has improved to 20/100; and by two years, the child can see almost as well as an adult (Courage & Adams, 1990).

D Despite their visual immaturity, newborns spend a lot of time actively looking about. They scan the
40 world in an organised way and pause when their eyes encounter an object or some change in the visual field. They are particularly attracted to areas of high visual contrast, such as the edges of an object. Instead of scanning the entire object, as an adult
45 would, they keep looking at areas that have the most edges. They also prefer complex patterns to plain ones, prefer patterns with curved lines to patterns with straight lines, and they are especially interested in faces (Franz, 1961). In an experiment on "visual
50 preferences", newborns as young as 10 hours to five days old were shown disks that differed in particular ways – a face like a circle, a bull's-eye, an array of fine print, and disks coloured white, yellow or red. Infants could tell the difference between them and looked
55 at different patterns for different lengths of time.

E The possibility that there is an inborn, unlearned preference for faces initially aroused great interest, but later research showed that infants are not attracted to faces per se but to stimulus characteristics such as
60 curved lines, high contrast, interesting edges, movement and complexity – all of which faces possess (Banks, Salapatek, 1983; Aslin, 1987). Newborns look mostly at the outside contour of a face, but by two months they focus on the inside of the face – the
65 eyes, nose and mouth (Haith, Bergman, & Moore, 1977). At this point parents notice with delight that the baby has begun to make eye contact.

Text 2–3: Hearing, taste and smell

Early human development

Hearing, taste and smell

F Newborn infants will startle at the sound of a loud noise. They will also turn their heads toward the source of a sound. Interestingly, the head-turning response disappears at about six weeks and does not reemerge until three or four months of age, at which time the infants will also search with their eyes for the source of the sound.

G The temporary disappearance of the head-turning response probably represents a maturational transition from a reflexive response controlled by subcortical areas of the brain to a voluntary attempt to locate the sound source. By four
10 months, they will reach in the correct direction toward the source of sound in the dark; by six months, they show a marked increase in their responsiveness to sounds that are accompanied by interesting sights and are able to pinpoint the
15 location of sound more precisely, an ability that continues to improve into their second year (Hillier, Hewitt & Morrongiello, 1992; Ashmead et al., 1991; Field, 1987).

H Newborn infants can also detect the difference
20 between very similar sounds, such as two tones that are only one note apart on the musical scale (Bridger, 1961), and they can distinguish sounds of the human voice from other kinds of sounds. We will see in Chapter 9 that they can also
25 distinguish a number of critical characteristics of human speech. For example, one-month-old infants can tell the difference between such similar sounds as "pa" and "ba". Interestingly, infants can distinguish between some speech
30 sounds better than adults. These are sounds that adults "hear" as identical because they are not distinguished in their native language (Aslin, Pisoni & Jusczyk, 1983). By six months of age, the child will have picked up enough information about the
35 language that it will also have begun to "screen out" sounds it does not use (Kuhl et al., 1992). Thus, human infants appear to be born with perceptual mechanisms already tuned to the properties of human speech that will help them
40 in their mastery of language (Eimas, 1975).

I Infants can discriminate differences in taste shortly after birth. They prefer sweet-tasting liquids to those that are salty, bitter, sour or bland. The characteristic response of the newborn to a
45 sweet liquid is a relaxed expression resembling a slight smile, sometimes accompanied by lip-licking. A sour solution produces pursed lips and a wrinkled nose. In response to a bitter solution, the baby will open its mouth with
50 the corners turned down and stick out its tongue in what appears to be an expression of disgust.

J Newborns can also discriminate among odours. They will turn their heads toward a sweet smell,
55 and their heart rate and respiration will slow down, indicating attention. Noxious odours, such as ammonia or rotten eggs, cause them to turn their heads away; heart rate and respiration accelerate, indicating distress. Infants
60 are even able to discriminate subtle differences in smells. After nursing for only a few days, an infant will consistently turn its head toward a pad saturated with its mother's milk in preference to one saturated with another
65 mother's milk (Russell, 1976). Only breast-fed babies show this ability to recognise the mother's odour (Cernoch & Porter, 1985). When bottle-fed babies are given a choice between their familiar formula and the smell
70 of a lactating breast, they will choose the latter (Porter et al., 1992). Thus, there seems to be an innate preference for the odour of breast milk. In general, the ability to distinguish among smells has a clear adaptive value:
75 it helps infants avoid noxious substances, thereby increasing their likelihood of survival.

Atkinson, R.L. et al., *Hilgard's Introduction to Psychology*, 13th edition (1999) pp. 70–71. © 1996.

ENVIRONMENT **TODAY**

ACID RAIN IN NORWAY

Although some of the effects of acidic deposits from the atmosphere – so-called 'acid rain' – were identified nearly 150 years ago, the 5 problem was only recognised as an international issue in the 1960s. This was when researchers in Scandinavia suggested that much of the enhanced acidity precipitation falling there was 10 due to the long-range transport of pollutants from other countries. Transboundary transport of pollution is now a widely accepted idea, and a number of international efforts 15 to combat the problem have been launched. *Environment Today* in this issue looks at the situation in Norway, where the acidification of freshwater ecosystems has shown 20 some improvement in recent years.

Damage to rivers and lakes

Sulphur dioxide (SO_2) and nitrogen oxides (NO and NO_2, collectively referred to as NO_x) have deleterious 25 effects on many parts of the environment on which they are deposited. They have adverse effects on human health, and on the growth of green plants, in which they inhibit photo-30 synthesis. Acid rain also damages buildings, corroding paint and metals and accelerating the weathering of some building stones. In Norway the cost of this type of damage to build-35 ings is estimated to be NOK 200–300 million (£16–24 million) each year.

The effects of acid rain on soil and water depend upon their natural 'buffering capacity' – the ability of 40 soil and water to neutralise incoming acids. This buffering capacity is largely determined by the nature of the bedrock: ecosystems on hard, impervious igneous or metamorphic 45 rock, with low calcium and magnesium contents, are most at risk of acidification from acid rain. All environments can withstand acid input up to a certain level – the 'critical 50 load', but beyond that level significant changes occur.

Perhaps the most notable acid rain damage in Norway has been to freshwater ecosystems. The death of 55 fish is one of the most reliable indicators of acidification. Fish die for two main reasons. When acidification reaches a certain level, young fish fresh from the spawn cannot 60 survive. Different species have different levels of tolerance, but the most sensitive are trout and salmon. The presence of aluminium is another common cause of fish death. 65 Aluminium ions are washed out of soils and rocks by incoming hydrogen ions in acid rain, and aluminium is toxic to fish because it prevents them from absorbing salts and 70 destroys their gills.

One study of 1,679 lakes in the south of the country in the 1970s found that brown trout were absent or had only sparse populations in 75 more than half the lakes. The proportion of lakes with no fish at all increased with declining pH levels (i.e. increasing levels of acidity). From 1960 to 1990, areas in southern 80 Norway where fish stocks have been damaged have increased fivefold.

Figure 1: Lime used to reduce acidification damage in Norway

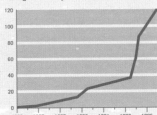

Text 3a–1: Acid rain in Norway cont.

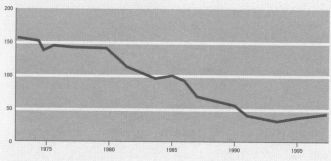

Figure 2: Emissions of sulphur dioxide in Norway

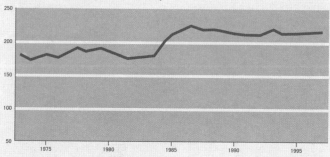

Figure 3: Emissions of nitrogen oxides in Norway

Combating acid rain damage

These depressing statistics of acid rain damage in Norway, largely concen- [85] trated in southern parts of the country, have generated action on a number of fronts. One method used to deal with the problem of acidified waters in the short term is the application of lime, [90] to increase pH and reduce acid levels. In Norway, the use of lime has increased rapidly since the early 1980s, and in the mid-1990s about 120,000 tonnes were applied (Figure [95] 1). In 1995, lime was applied in more than 2,500 locations, covering a precipitation area of about 6,400 km². However, lime can only repair acidification damage to a certain degree. It [100] will never be a permanent solution

In the long term, reduction of acid rain damage can only be achieved by reducing emissions of acid rain compounds at their source. To achieve [105] these aims, a number of international agreements have been reached and, under these agreements, Norway has made three main political pledges:

- [110] to reduce sulphur dioxide emissions to 76% of the 1980 level.
- to stabilise oxides of nitrogen emissions at the 1987 level.
- to reduce oxides of nitrogen emissions to 70% of the 1986 level.

[115] On the sulphur dioxide front, Norway has almost achieved its aim already (Figure 2). Between 1980 and 1995, sulphur dioxide emissions were reduced by 75% due to increased taxes [120] on sulphur in oils and a reduction in the sulphur content of light heating oils and diesel. Efforts to reduce emissions of nitrogen oxides have not been so successful (Figure 3). After an [125] increase in emissions of 29% from 1980 to 1987, they were reduced by 5% in the period 1987–1995, and Norway remains one of the highest emitters of nitrogen oxides in Europe when meas- [130] ured in per capita terms. The goal of reducing emissions to 70% of the 1986 level seems unlikely to be achieved.

However, important though the efforts in Norway are, the fact remains [135] that most of the acid rain falling on the country is emitted by other countries. No less than 95% of the sulphur deposited on Norway, and 86% of the nitrogen compounds, is due to long- [140] range transboundary air pollution. Emissions from Great Britain and Germany, for example, each contribute more pollution to the Norwegian environment than domestic sources. [145] Emissions from these and other countries are however also being reduced. The sulphur content of precipitation falling on Norway has fallen by more than 40% since 1980, and the goals set [200]

[150] for countries by the Sulphur Protocol of 1994 aim to reduce it still further.

The 1994 Sulphur Protocol was a milestone in international pollution control in that it was based on the crit- [155] ical loads approach and assigned different levels of reduction to different countries, aiming to bring about environmental improvements at the lowest possible cost. Britain, for example, has [160] committed to an 80% reduction in emissions by the year 2010 from the baseline year of 1980, while Germany's commitment is 87%. Most countries reached their reduction tar- [165] gets by the year 2000, but for some the full reductions will not be reached before 2010. The benefits of these reductions for Norway are already being felt. While 30% of Norwegian [170] territory received amounts of sulphur that exceeded the critical load in 1985, this figure has been reduced by 25% by 1990 and should be cut to 16% by 2010 (Table 1).

Table 1: Excess deposits of sulphur in Norway	
Year	Area where critical load exceeded (% national land area)
1985	30%
1995	25%
2010	16%

[175] Although there is no doubt that the acid rain problem in Norway, and elsewhere in Europe, is being tackled, one lesson of this is clear: preventing acid rain damage and rehabilitating [180] affected ecosystems is a long-term exercise. For some acidified lakes, researchers believe that it might take more than 100 years before fresh waters regain something close to [185] their original species composition with stable and maintained functions.

References

- Mason, C.F. (1996), *Biology of Freshwater Pollution*, 3rd edn, Longman.
- [190] Morecroft, M. (1995), 'Air pollution and the nitrogen cycle,' *Geography Review*, Vol. 9, No 2, pp. 7–10.
- Whyatt, D. and Metcalf, S. (1995), 'Sulphur emissions and acid rain,' [195] *Geography Review*, Vol. 9, No 1, pp. 14–18.

NICK MIDDLETON

Nick Middleton *is a Lecturer in Physical Geography at St. Anne's and Oriel Colleges, Oxford University. His special interests* [200] *include drylands and environmental issues.*

Source: Middleton, N., 'Acid Rain in Norway' in *Geography Review*, Vol. 11, No. 4. (1998)

SKYLARKS IN DECLINE

The skylark is one of Britain's commonest birds, yet its population on farmland may have fallen by nearly 60% in just over 20 years. If we are to stop this decline, and hopefully reverse it, we need to understand the underlying causes, and to study the ecology of the species.

Where do we get our facts from? Britain and Ireland can be divided into 3,862 10km x 10km squares, and data on bird distribution are held by the British Trust for Ornithology (BTO), an organisation concerned primarily with long-term surveys, population work and ringing and migration studies. From time to time, distribution records of different groups are published. When *The Atlas of Breeding Birds in Britain and Ireland* was published in 1976 it revealed that the skylark was the most widespread bird in Britain and Ireland – present in 98% of the 10km squares. Skylarks were known to breed in 86% of the squares in which they were recorded and probably bred in the other 14%.

The total skylark population in Britain and Ireland in 1976 was estimated to be between two and four million pairs, on the assumption that each 10km square would hold between 500 and 1,000 breeding pairs. However, this involved some degree of informed guesswork because skylarks live in such a wide variety of open habitats with low vegetation (mainly grasslands, but also heaths, moors, salt marshes and farmland) and relatively little was known about population densities outside farmland.

During 1988–1991 there was a repeat scheme published as *The New Atlas of Breeding Birds in Britain and Ireland*. When the number of 10km squares occupied was compared with those occupied in 1968–72, it revealed that skylarks had lost a small amount of ground – about 3%. The new scheme's more detailed work on the numbers of birds produced a more reliable estimate for the skylark population, concluding that there were about two million pairs in Britain and a further 570,000 in Ireland. It might seem that the estimate of 2.57 million pairs fits within the earlier estimate, but when we look at the part of the survey for which we have most detail, a different story emerges.

Decline on lowland farms

The only detailed evidence we have of any decline concerns skylarks on lowland farmland. We have no firm evidence for other habitats, and it is most important to remember this when discussing falling skylark numbers. We know that on lowland farmland (which the *New Atlas* shows as having the highest densities of breeding skylarks) the breeding population has fallen by about 58% over a 20-year period (see Figure 1). This huge decline has been mirrored in other common farmland birds, including grey partridge, turtle dove, barn owl and corn bunting. The source of our evidence is the BTO's long-running *Common Birds Census*. Repeated annually, the census uses a mapping technique to produce a year-by-year index for all the species involved, calculated against a 'reference' or 'datum' year (1980) where the index is given an arbitrary value of 100. The indices provide a handy way of plotting the population ups and downs of a large number of species and, importantly, of identifying longer-term trends.

Text 3a–2: Skylarks in decline cont.

Figure 1: *Common Bird Census* indices for Skylark, 1962–1994

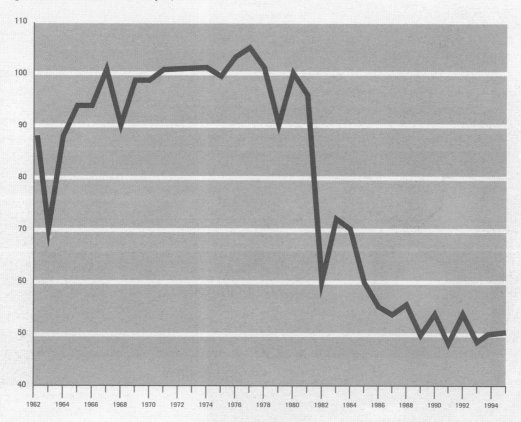

Possible reasons for the decline

95 It is clear that something has gone badly wrong for farmland birds during the last 20–25 years. To find out what has happened to the sky-lark, and why, and also to investi-
100 gate means of putting the situation right, the Royal Society for the Protection of Birds has begun a new research programme. It is like-ly that what we learn about skylarks
105 will have some relevance to other farmland species too.

Most of us only see skylarks singing high in the sky. They build a simple grass-lined nest among
110 grass or crops, and chicks and adults feed on seeds, leaves, worms, insects and larvae. There have been radical changes in agricultural prac-tices over the last 25 years and,
115 given what is already known about skylark ecology, it is reasonable to infer that these changes are impli-cated in its decline.

(1) Increased areas of cereals

120 It seems likely that the widespread change from mixed farming regimes to monoculture has had a profound effect on skylarks. The disappearance of grass meadows may have meant a
125 reduction in insect food available for chicks, for instance. Where a variety of crops were grown, skylarks could always find suitable nest-sites, and since cropping patterns and timing
130 varied so much they could enjoy a prolonged breeding season. Cereal monocultures, on the other hand, provide much less choice and are also only suitable for nesting for a very
135 short period. This timing problem has probably been made worse by the modern practice of autumn sowing – the crops become too dense for nest-sites very early in the season.
140 Autumn sowing has also led to the virtual disappearance of winter stub-bles, which we know were very important sources of skylark food in winter. Skylarks would almost cer-
145 tainly fare much better with more spring sowing, or at least a mixture of this and autumn sowing.

(2) Reduction of insect food by pesticides

150 Autumn sowing and the monocul-ture system depend on heavy appli-cations of pesticides. A combination of insecticides and herbicides proba-bly reduces insect food supplies both
155 for adult and young skylarks, and destroys many insect food plants. In addition, because pesticides are applied very early in the growth cycle with autumn-sown cereals, it is very
160 likely that insect food is greatly reduced by spring, when young sky-larks need it most.

(3) Reduction of insect food in intensively managed pastures

165 Intensively managed pastures, with high densities of grazing livestock and heavy applications of nitrogen fertilis-er to maximise the production of good grass, are bad news for skylarks,
170 and this is not just because more ani-mals means a greater chance of nests being trampled. The dense, uniform sward produced is not very good for nesting and carries far fewer insects
175 than old-fashioned pastureland.

ENVIRONMENT **TODAY**

A *A skylark nest in a Suffolk wheatfield.*

B *Skylark feeding her young.*

C *A skylark's nightmare! Cereal crops are aiding the decline.*

Designing a plan of action

We know already that skylarks fare better on mixed farmland, and also where organic farming is practised. 180 They do very well, too, on 'set-aside land', which is either land put out of crop production for several years, or fields or field margins from which no crop is taken for a year. Farmers are 185 compensated for setting land aside, and it can help to reduce some persistent weeds. We have a number of ideas about how the situation could be improved for skylarks elsewhere, 190 but we need to translate ideas and intuition into a programme supported by good science. For this reason, the RSPB has embarked upon a three-year research programme, investigat- 195 ing skylark ecology on 12 farms in three counties – four each in Norfolk, Oxfordshire and Dorset.

This gives a good regional spread to the work, but it also involves three 200 different categories of farm on predominantly arable land where cattle and sheep are reared, and in mixed farming areas.

If we are to begin to help sky- 205 larks, we must find out a great deal more about precisely what they need from a modern farming landscape. The research will tell us which habitats they feed in, both in summer 210 and in winter; exactly what adults and chicks eat; how breeding success varies on different crop types, and whether this varies from farm to farm and between regions; and, 215 hopefully, more about winter survival. In three years' time we hope that our action plan for skylark 240 conservation will be much improved by this new research input.

220 Further reading

- RSPB (1996) 'Crisis point,' *Birds*, the magazine of the RSPB, Vol. 16, Issue 3, pp 17–21.
- RSPB (1996), 'The Skylark', *Birds*, the 225 magazine of the RSPB, Vol. 16, Issue 3, pp 24–27.

MIKE EVERETT

Mike Everett *works for the Royal Society for the Protection of Birds (RSPB), Europe's* 230 *largest voluntary wildlife conservation organisation, with one million members. The RSPB's primary function is to conserve the UK's birds and their habitats, both through the promotion of more wildlife-friendly plan-* 235 *ning and land-use policies. The Society is increasingly involved with similar work overseas and is the UK partner of the global conservation body Birdlife International. Detailed investigation of the ecology of declin-* 240 *ing and Red List bird species is an important aspect of the Society's applied research.*

Source: Everett, M., 'Impact – Skylarks in decline' in *Biological Sciences Review*, Vol. 10, No. 2 (November 1997)

The Economist, Oct 7th, 1999

Ring in the new

The best thing about mobile phones is their convenience

The mobile-phone industry is full of people who are convinced they are changing the world. Mobile phones, those people say, are fundamentally revolutionising the way people work; they are giving individualism yet another shove; and they are ushering in something grandly called "the mobile information society".

Mobile phones undoubtedly make it easier for people to work wherever they choose. (An American advertisement features a man with a golf bag talking on his mobile phone, telling his boss that he is working from home.) They are a great help for people on the move, and they make it easier for people to get in touch with each other whenever they need to. They are quintessentially personal devices. Japanese teenagers used to have to phone each other at home, with the attendant risk that the phone would be answered by a grown-up; now they can chat to each other at all hours without being intercepted.

But these arguments provoke all sorts of questions. Do mobile phones really make workers more mobile, or is it workers' increased mobility that accounts for the spread of the devices? Do teenagers want cellphones because they are all arrant individualists, or is this just another example of conformity induced by mass marketing? And was the arrival of the mobile information society not attributed to the laptop computer and the Internet long before smart phones came along?

The claims about the changing nature of work are clearly exaggerated. Huge numbers of workers were mobile long before cellphones came along; on the other hand, some of the ties that tether people to their desks are much stronger than telephone wires. Five years ago TBWA Chiat/Day,

Ring in the new – the best thing about mobile phones is their convenience

an advertising agency, led the charge into the "virtual workplace" when its offices in Venice, California, proved too small for a fast-expanding workforce. The company gave everyone a mobile phone, a laptop and a locker, and told them to come into the office only when they needed to. The experiment proved a disaster: workers complained of isolation and lack of creative interaction. Last year the company traded virtual communication for the real thing, moving into large offices where everybody has their own desk, along with plenty of open spaces for informal meetings. TBWA Chiat/Day is only one of a huge number of companies to discover that people need to "share the same air" as well as to "share the airwaves."

Even more exaggerated are the claims about individualism. Arguably, the proliferation of cellphones reinforces group behaviour rather than individualism. Mostafa Terrab, Morocco's telephone regulator, says Moroccan immigrants in Europe rely heavily on mobile phones to keep in contact with their families back home. The mobile phone, he says, is "the virtual family nucleus" of a largely illiterate society. The teenagers who have embraced the devices use them mainly to reinforce their social networks. They are forever phoning each other to rearrange meetings as they wander around Tokyo or Helsinki—and each ring of the phone adds to their popularity count.

Having a cellphone "is like having someone beside you all the time", one Japanese woman told a local newspaper.

What about the mobile information society? Certainly airport lounges are full of people desperate to log on to the Internet, suggesting a huge potential demand for phones that will allow them to do that with less bother and no wires. But much of what the mobile-phone industry is offering is not really new; it is just an easier way of doing things that people are doing already, from checking their e-mail to paying bills wherever they are. Pekka Palin, one of the founders of WapIT, points out that many mobile-phone users do not want the sort of sophisticated services that a "mobile information society" entails. They want old-fashioned things like horoscopes and jokes.

Less stress

Perhaps the most obvious attraction of mobile phones is too simple to catch the gurus' attention: they make life easier. Once people have them, they no longer need to hike along the motorway when their car breaks down, or twiddle their thumbs when a friend they are meeting is unavoidably delayed, or feed coins into a payphone only to have them eaten up. Mobiles allow their users to avoid frustration, and fill "niche time" that would otherwise be wasted.

Being constantly in touch is particularly beneficial for three groups of people. The first are itinerant bosses. Because of the current fashion for companies to contract out everything but their core businesses and hand as much power as possible to front-line workers, bosses now spend much more time establishing relations with potential business partners than telling their employees what to do. Mobile phones make that relationship-building easier. The second group are the vast army of people who spend their time either on the road or at clients' offices rather than sitting at their own desk. These range from high-powered consultants to today's travelling salesmen. Booz Allen & Hamilton, a consultancy, used to present people with a briefcase when they signed on with the firm; now it presents them with a PC and a mobile phone. Mark Feighner, a top manager at GTE, one of America's largest wireless networks, emphasises the importance of a third group of people on the move who are often overlooked: blue-collar workers. When countries start to move over to mobile phones, taxi drivers and plumbers are among the first to pile in. Many mobile work teams are also likely to be early adopters of Internet phones. House-builders, for example, will be able to check the specifications of houses over the Internet rather than trudge back to the office.

But mobile phones do not just follow their owners around; they also know

The Economist, Oct 7th, 1999

where those owners are at any one time. That means they can be used to provide an extraordinary range of local services.

There are few better places to study such services than the offices of Sunday, one of Hong Kong's most innovative cellular operators. The offices are built in the sort of aggressively modernist style you would expect from a mobile-phone company. In the lobby sit busts of three 20th-century giants: Sun Yat-sen, John Kennedy and Mahatma Gandhi. (The company used all three in its advertisements celebrating the arrival of "number portability".) The office is full of people who look as if they are barely out of university. The company's boss, Craig Ehrlich, a displaced Angelino who is apologetic about his native country's backwardness in wireless technology, explains the huge range of "location-based" services his company offers.

When Sunday customers enter a shopping mall, they can dial a number to find out about special offers. Their phones will tell them about deals on anything from meals to Gucci loafers. The information is updated throughout the day. When customers run out of petrol or break a heel, they dial another number to find the nearest garage or cobbler. Yet another number lets them find out what is on at the local cinema, and reserve tickets if they wish. Sunday also offers a sophisticated dating service. Customers feed their details into a computer alongside those of

thousands of other Sunday customers. When someone matching their requirements enters the bar where they are having a drink, their phone rings and asks if they would like to go over and talk to the potential date.

This service clearly has the power to target advertising much more precisely, and thus make it more effective. Many of Sunday's customers are happy to receive ads over the phone – either by voice or by text – in return for the chance of getting a bargain. These ads are a marketing man's dream. They can be adjusted to fit the customer's demographic profile, and can be sent when the customer is in the best possible place for buying a product. They can also be monitored so that the advertisers know how customers are responding. "Advertisers can reach the exact people they want to reach," says Mr Ehrlich, "in the exact spot where they want to reach them – and they can often get an immediate response."

Six months after the launch of its advertising service, Sunday gets only 1% of its total income from this source. But Mr Ehrlich thinks it will become far more important in future. Advertisers will develop much closer relationships with mobile-phone companies. For example, they may start subsidising mobile phones – or even give them away free – in the way that some companies are now giving away computers. Mobile-phone companies may begin to realise that their most precious resource

is not the airwaves but the attention of the customers who carry their products around with them.

Wireless devices are also likely to have a big impact on another industry: transport. Car companies are beginning to incorporate wireless gadgets in their products just as routinely as they now incorporate computer microchips. General Motors' advertisements trumpet the fact that its cars are fitted with the "On Star" safety feature, which sends a signal to the rescue services if their car runs into trouble. Mercedes-Benz, BMW and Jaguar have struck deals with Motorola to furnish their cars with similar devices. Volvo's racing cars are fitted with wireless gadgets that keep the pit stop informed about the car's condition and location, so the mechanics can start fixing the car the moment it comes into the pits. Most truck companies track their fleet by either cellular or satellite equipment so that they know exactly where each truck is and what shape it is in.

So far and yet so near

These smart vehicles will be just one part of a much bigger wireless business: telemetry. People have used wireless devices for years to monitor expensive pieces of machinery in isolated places. But now that wireless can deliver the Internet, such monitoring is about to get a huge boost. The Yankee Group predicts that most machines above a certain value will be fitted

Ring in the new – the best thing about mobile phones is their convenience

with telemetry units so that people can keep an eye on their performance, and that this technology will become much more pervasive in future. Wireless devices can be used to monitor anything from utility meters (thus getting rid of meter readers) to Coke machines (so they can be filled up just before they run out). They can be used to signal whether a building is being broken into or pollution has reached a critical level. They can also be used to deliver instructions to other devices: lock yourself out of your car, for example, and you can use your mobile phone to tell the doors to open.

Most pervasively of all, the mobile-phone companies want to change the way people use and manage their money. The idea is to turn phones into both electronic wallets and portable ATMs. The Internet will allow people to manage their bank accounts while on the move. Smart cards will allow them to load their phones with electronic cash. And wireless receivers in, say, vending machines and parking meters will allow them to dial a number and add their purchases to their phone bill. The aim is not simply to grab new business, though that is obviously important; it is to reinforce the customer's relationship with his mobile phone, turning it into the one item that he cannot do without.

The country that has travelled furthest down this road is Finland. The Finns can already use their mobile phones to pay for Pepsi-Cola from vending machines and songs from juke boxes, not to mention car washes and golf balls; once the technology has proved itself, the country's biggest cellular network, Sonera, is planning to move on to more expensive items. Finnish banks also rushed to embrace mobile communications when the steep recession of the early 1990s forced them to shed large numbers of staff. Okobank, the main bank for 2.1m Finns, allows its customers to use their mobile phones not only to monitor and manage their accounts but also to make payments. It uses the same technology to keep in contact with its customers, sending them reminders if their accounts hit certain agreed "triggers" (too much or too little money), and keeping them informed about the services they offer (if they buy travellers' cheques, for example, they might receive information about travel insurance).

Other countries are following in Finland's footsteps. HSBC's Hong Kong branches are among several banks there that plan to allow their customers to manage their bank accounts and trade shares over the airwaves. "About 3m people have mobile phones, compared with only 1m who have access to the Internet," HSBC's Darren Sugden points out. "People have their mobile phones with them all the time—and they have a very personal relationship with them." Hong Kong's Jockey Club allows people to place bets over its private network, using various wireless devices. According to Steve Beason, the club's director of information technology, a good proportion of the money bet on its races is "cashless, wireless and operatorless".

If mobiles make life so much more fun and so much easier, at a cost that is constantly diminishing, they are clearly too good to be true. And indeed critics are finding plenty of things wrong with them.

The Economist, Oct 9th, 2003

Beyond the bubble

After its spectacular crash, the telecoms industry is still picking itself off the floor. But provided it can adjust to less dizzying expectations, the business still offers plenty of opportunities, says Tom Standage.

Note: Only the last part of the article 'Beyond the bubble' is given. It looks at future trends in the telecoms industry.

Beyond the bubble - future trends in the telecoms industry

Now what?

The post-bubble opportunities seem to lie in exploiting three main trends. The most visible growth area is the continuing rise of mobile phones, which have overtaken fixed-line phones to become the most widespread communications devices on earth. Their number is expected to rise from 1.3 billion today to 2 billion by 2007, and they are being increasingly used to do much more than make phone calls, providing new opportunities for wireless operators and equipment makers.

The second trend is the growth of high-speed or "broadband" Internet access, which is booming in many parts of the world. This offers a valuable new market for fixed-line operators, once they have supercharged their existing telephone networks to make them broadband-capable.

A third promising area is in the corporate-telecoms market. As large firms look for ways to cut costs and move operations overseas, many are adopting new Internet-based technologies that can interconnect regional offices cheaply and securely and allow voice and data to flow over the same network. Many operators are now overhauling and simplifying their tangled networks to ensure they can implement such "next-generation services" quickly and efficiently.

But all three areas involve difficult transitions for telecoms operators. The continued health of the mobile-telephony industry depends on being able to deliver data services alongside voice calls, revenues from which are flat or declining. Creating and delivering multimedia services to mobile handsets is, however, proving to be a lot more complicated than simply providing telephony. Similarly, fixed-line operators offering broadband Internet connections are having to work harder to provide both data and voice services rather than voice services alone. And in the corporate market the operators face a new challenge: the increasing overlap between telecoms and information technology (IT). If they are to offer next-generation services such as Internet hosting or call-centre outsourcing, network operators must beef up their expertise in IT or form partnerships with systems integrators.

Equipment vendors also face a wrenching transition. Mobile, broadband and next-generation services require new equipment on the edges of telecoms networks, rather than more capacity in the network core, which is where so much unnecessary investment was made during the bubble. This has completely changed infrastructure spending patterns, and equipment vendors have had to adjust.

In short, there are still opportunities in telecoms – but not where they were during the boom. The experience of the past couple of years, says Dave Dorman, chief executive of AT&T, has demonstrated that there is more to being a telecoms operator than simply owning a shiny new network. The best prospects are at the network's edges, not at its core, and revolve around providing complex services, not merely dumb capacity. The watchword now is transformation, not construction. Only by embracing this new reality will the industry find a way out of its troubles.

STATISTICS

◆◆◆

WITHOUT TEARS

SECTION 1

MAKING SENSE OF EXPERIENCE

It is by making sense of our experience that we human beings grow wiser and gain greater control over the environment we live in. This has been true for the development of the human race over the centuries. It is equally true for each of us as individuals in our own lifetimes. Fortunately, we
5 have this capacity for noticing things. We observe people, things and events in the world around us. We notice their similarities and differences, their patterns and regularities – especially when such features could endanger us or, alternatively, be turned to our advantage.

Many of our observations involve us in counting and measuring.
10 Perhaps we do so in rough-and-ready fashion, and often so intuitively that we are scarcely aware of this habit of 'quantification'. Nevertheless our observations and comparisons are often in terms of 'how much?', 'how big?', 'how often?', 'how far?', 'how difficult?', 'how quickly?', 'how well?', and so on.

15 Sometimes our observations concern a single thing or person or event. For example, we may notice the size of the potato-crop in a particular field this year. We may make several observations about the same thing: not only the size of the crop in this field but also how much fertilizer was used, the nature of the soil, how much sunshine and rain it had, etc.
20 Sometimes our observations concern several similar but different things. For example, we may observe the size of the potato-crop in several different fields this year, or in the same field over a succession of years.

Thus, we may make one or more observations on one individual, or we may do so for several individuals. Soon we have a *collection* of
25 observations (or 'DATA', to use the technical jargon).

Inquisitively, as if by instinct, we start looking at connections and patterns, similarities and differences, among the things we happen to have noticed. We ask ourselves questions about the data.

For example, what questions might we ask in looking for connections
30 among the data we have collected about the size of potato-crops?

STATISTICS WITHOUT TEARS – MAKING SENSE OF EXPERIENCE

SECTION 2

We might ask: is the size of the crop similar in all fields this year? Or, is it similar in this field from one year to another? If not, why not? What else is different about those fields, or years, that might explain the differences?

35 All such questions lead to an even more vital one: what can we learn from the connections we see among this collection of data that might help us act more effectively in the future?

This is where statistics comes in. It has been developed as a way of making sense of collections of observations. It aims, particularly, to help us avoid jumping to conclusions and to be cautious about the extent to 40 which we can *generalize* from our always limited experience.

The tendency to generalize is an essential part of our everyday thinking. Because this particular field was generously treated with a certain fertilizer and gave a bigger than usual potato-crop, we may feel inclined to generalize and suggest that, therefore, *other* fields so treated 45 would give bigger than usual potato-crops.

Would you think it safe to generalize in this way – on the basis of experience with one field? Why, or why not?

STATISTICS WITHOUT TEARS – MAKING SENSE OF EXPERIENCE

SECTION 3

In fact, such a generalization would be rather dangerous – it is very likely to be wrong. The bigger crop may be due not to the fertilizer but to, say, the weather. (That is, we may have jumped to an incorrect conclusion.) So even the same field, treated in the same way with fertilizer, may give a very different yield in another year. And as for the other fields, they may differ in yet other ways that could influence the potato-yield, e.g. type of soil, crop grown in the previous year, prevalence of plant disease in neighbouring fields, and so on. (Hence the weakness in our generalization.)

So, what is true of one field in one year may not be true of the same field in other years, let alone of other fields. If we want to generalize more confidently, we need more experience – more observations. The more fields we look at, and over more and more years, the more confident we can be in suggesting how the potato-crop is likely to turn out in other, similar fields.

But notice the word 'likely' in the sentence above. 'Likelihood' or 'weighing up the chances' (that is, PROBABILITY) is central to the statistical view of the world. It recognizes no 100% certainties, especially when dealing with individual people, things or events. For example, a particular kind of field may, *in general*, produce a bigger potato-crop if treated in a certain way, but there will be many exceptions.

In which of these two cases would you think me more likely to be proved correct:

(a) If I predict that fields of a certain type will, in general, produce a bigger crop if treated in such-and-such a way? or
(b) If I predict that any such *particular* field you care to pick out will do so?

STATISTICS WITHOUT TEARS – MAKING SENSE OF EXPERIENCE

SECTION 4

75 I'd be more likely to be correct in (a) than in (b). While such fields in general (maybe nine out of ten of them) will behave as expected, I can't be sure that any one particular field you happen to choose will be one of those that do.

As you will learn, statistics helps us to look for reliable regularities 80 and associations among things 'in general' and 'in the long run'. At the same time, however, it teaches us proper caution in expecting these to hold true of any particular individuals. The two chief concerns of statistics are with (1) summarizing our experience so that we and other people can understand its essential features, and (2) using the summary 85 to make estimates or predictions about what is likely to be the case in other (perhaps future) situations.

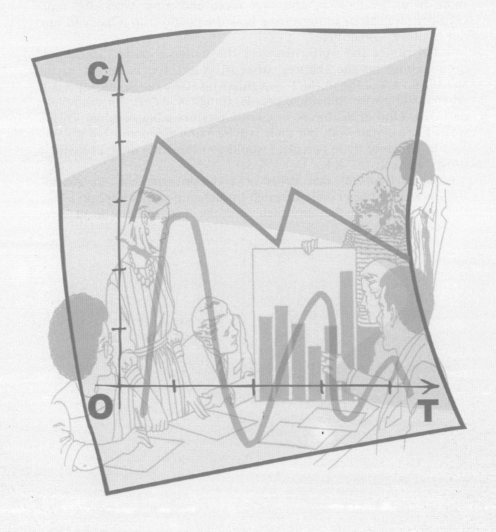

SECTION 5

WHAT IS STATISTICS?

Before we go any further, we'd better take note, in passing, that the word 'statistics' is used in at least four different senses. First of all, it can indicate, very broadly, a whole *subject* or *discipline*, and everything that gets studied or practised in its name. Secondly, and more specifically, the
5 term may refer to the *methods* used to collect or process or interpret quantitative data. Thirdly, the term may be applied to *collections of data* gathered by those methods. And fourthly, it may refer to certain *specially calculated figures* (e.g. an average) that somehow characterize such a collection of data. Thus, to illustrate the four meanings in turn,
10 a researcher in a firm's *statistics* department may use *statistics* (statistical methods) to gather and interpret *statistics* (data) about the revenue from sales of a new detergent, and may summarize his findings by quoting the *statistics* of 'average sales per thousand of population' in various towns and 'range of sales revenue from town to town'.

15   The meaning I shall emphasize in this book is the second of those mentioned above: statistics as a set of *methods of inquiry*. It is these methods that enable us to think statistically – a very powerful way to think – about a variety of situations that involve measurements or observations of quantities.

20   Few professional activities are untouched by statistical thinking, and most academic disciplines use it to a greater or lesser degree. Its applications in science, especially the 'biological sciences' like genetics, medicine and psychology, are both numerous and well known. But the physical sciences (e.g. meteorology, engineering and physics) also need
25 statistical methods. And even in the humanities, the dating of ancient fragments of textile or pottery has been revolutionized by the essentially statistical technique of radio-carbon dating; while statistical methods have also been used in literary studies to help decide such questions as whether a particular author wrote a certain work, or at
30 what point in his lifetime it was written. Statistics has developed out of an aspect of our everyday thinking to become a ubiquitous tool of systematic research.

  But it is time we got down to discussing what it is about statistical thinking that can lend itself to such a variety of pursuits. Statistics
35 arises out of caution in the face of uncertainty. Statistical thinking is a way of recognizing that our observations of the world can never be totally accurate; they are always somewhat uncertain. For instance, a child we record as being four feet in height will not be exactly that – somewhere between 3 feet $11\frac{1}{2}$ inches and 4 feet $\frac{1}{2}$ inch maybe, but not

STATISTICS WITHOUT TEARS – WHAT IS STATISTICS?

40 exactly four feet. And the chance of inaccuracy is even greater if we use our present observations to estimate what observations elsewhere might reveal. Thus, we might want to use our knowledge that four feet is the average height in this child's class to predict the average height in another class.

45   In such matters there can be no certainty. But statistics enables us to estimate the extent of our errors. Thus, we may express near certainty that the child's height lies within a range of four feet plus or minus half an inch; or we may calculate that the chances are ninety-nine in a hundred that the average height in another class 50 lies within two inches of four feet.

STATISTICS WITHOUT TEARS – DESCRIPTIVE AND INFERENTIAL STATISTICS

SECTION 6

DESCRIPTIVE AND INFERENTIAL STATISTICS

You will find that statistics textbooks commonly make a distinction between (1) DESCRIPTIVE STATISTICS (methods used to summarize or describe our observations), and (2) INFERENTIAL STATISTICS (using those observations as a basis for making estimates or predictions, i.e. inferences about a
5 situation that has not yet been observed).

Look again at those three 'everyday' statements I mentioned earlier. Which of them appear(s) 'descriptive' and which 'inferential', in the sense indicated above?

(i)   'On average, I cycle about 100 miles a week';
10 (ii)   'We can expect a lot of rain at this time of year';
(iii)   'The earlier you start revising, the better you are likely to do in the exam'.

STATISTICS WITHOUT TEARS – DESCRIPTIVE AND INFERENTIAL STATISTICS

SECTION 7

Statement (i) is descriptive (an attempt to summarize experience), while (ii) and (iii) go beyond what is likely to happen in the future.

15   The distinction between descriptive and inferential statistics depends upon another: the distinction between *samples* and *populations*.

In statistical jargon, 'POPULATION' does not necessarily refer to a body of people. It may refer to people, but it may equally well refer to white mice, to light-bulbs of a particular brand, to substandard dwellings in 20 inner Birmingham, to meteorites, to future examination results in British secondary schools, and so on. The point is that population refers to *all* the cases or situations that the 'statistician' wants his inferences or guesses or estimates to apply to. Thus, different statisticians may be making inferences about the learning ability of (all) white mice; 25 predicting how long all light-bulbs of a particular type are likely to burn; estimating the cost of renovating (all) substandard dwellings; predicting the composition of (all) meteorites; guessing the (total) numbers of candidates passing various examinations, and so on.

Perhaps it is also worth pointing out that the researcher will not be 30 interested in every aspect of members of a population. Rather, he is interested in just some – maybe only one – of the many attributes or characteristics that members might have in common. Thus a psychologist may not be concerned to speculate about the tail-length or litter-size of white mice (though these characteristics might interest 35 other researchers); he is interested simply in their learning ability. Neither might the astrophysicist be interested in predicting the geographical distribution or the size of falling meteorites as well as their composition.

However, even if he is interested in only one characteristic of his 40 population, the researcher will be most likely to study all members of it. Usually he has to do the best he can with a SAMPLE – a relatively small selection – from within the population. Often he must do this to save time and expense. For the astrophysicist to tour the world inspecting every meteorite that has ever been known to fall would be prohibitively 45 expensive. Again, an industrial researcher who is estimating the burning-life of a brand of light bulb by 'testing to destruction' cannot test all the population or there will be none left to sell.

In some cases, it may be logically impossible to study all members of the population. The population may be infinite, or simply not yet 50 available for study. Thus, the psychologist who is studying learning ability in white mice will hope his results, and therefore his inferences, will have some application to all white mice – not just the millions that exist at this moment but also the further millions not yet born. He may even

STATISTICS WITHOUT TEARS – DESCRIPTIVE AND INFERENTIAL STATISTICS

hope his results can be generalized to explain *human* learning. Likewise,
55 the astrophysicist may well use his statistics to generalize not just about
the meteorites that have already fallen to earth, or even about those that
will fall in future; he may hope to speculate also about the composition
of other objects flying around in space.

All such researchers go *beyond* the available information. They
60 generalize from a sample to a population, from the seen to the unseen.
(So do we all, though often in a rather careless, uncontrolled way, when
using everyday 'common sense'.) This idea of generalizing from a
sample applies to research in the arts as well as in the sciences. For
example, one would not have to have read everything ever written by,
65 say, D.H. Lawrence and Joseph Conrad before one could begin
generalizing about how they compared and contrasted as novelists. One
could work from a sample of two or three books by each author.

Anyway, *descriptive* statistics is concerned with summarizing or
describing a sample. *Inferential* statistics is concerned with generalizing
70 from a sample, to make estimates and inferences about a wider population. Consider a biologist experimenting with the feeding of chicks. He
may report (using descriptive statistics) that particular samples of 60
chicks, fed a particular compound, grow faster than a similar sample fed
on some standard diet. So much (the weight gain) he reports as fact. But
75 he goes beyond fact. He uses inferential statistics to suggest that *all*
similar chicks (the wider population) would grow faster if given
similar treatment.

How safe are such generalizations from a part to a whole? Well,
that is largely what statistics is about: quantifying the probability of
80 error. We will be looking at the underlying ideas in subsequent chapters.
One thing we can say at this stage, however: the reliability of the
generalization will depend on how well the sample mirrors the
population – in other words: is the sample truly representative of
the population?

Source: Rowntree, D., *Statistics Without Tears*, Penguin, (1982) pp. 14–21

COMMON QUESTIONS ABOUT
CLIMATE CHANGE

• United Nations Environment Programme •
• World Meteorological Organization •

The scientists listed below have volunteered their time to write and review this brochure. The brochure is cosponsored by the United Nations Environment Programme and the World Meteorological Organization. In addition, the United Nations Environment Programme, the National Oceanic and Atmospheric Administration, the U.S. Global Change Research Program and the Rockefeller Brothers Fund contributed funds for the layout and printing of the brochure. Leonie Haimson and Christine Ennis assisted in editing and Elizabeth C. Johnston and Julianne Snider designed the layout of the brochure.

AUTHORS
- Steven R Hamburg
  Brown University, USA
- Neil Harris
  European Ozone Research Coordinating Unit, UK
- Jill Jaeger
  International Institute for Applied Systems Analysis, Austria
- Thomas R. Karl
  National Oceanic and Atmospheric Administration, USA
- Mack McFarland
  *United Nations Environment Programme
  (on loan from the DuPont Company), Kenya*
- John R B. Mitchell
  Hadley Centre for Climate Prediction & Research, UK
- Michael Oppenheimer
  Environmental Defense Fund, USA
- Benjamin D. Santer
  Lawrence Livermore National Laboratory, USA
- Stephen Schneider
  Stanford University, USA
- Kevin E. Trenberth
  National Center for Atmospheric Research, USA
- Tom M.L. Wigley
  National Center for Atmospheric Research, USA

REVIEWERS/CONTRIBUTORS
- Daniel L. Albritton
  National Oceanic and Atmospheric Administration, USA
- Bert Bolin
  *Chairman of the Intergovernmental Panel on Climate
  Change, Sweden*
- Theresa Cookro
  National Oceanic and Atmospheric Administration, USA
- Susana B. Diaz
  Ozone and UV Laboratory, CADIC/CONICET, Argentina

- Robert E. Dickinson
  University of Arizona, USA
- Christine A. Ennis
  National Oceanic and Atmospheric Administration, USA
- Paul J. Fraser
  *Commonwealth Scientific and Industrial Research
  Organization, Australia*
- Hartmut Grassl
  World Meteorological Organization, Switzerland
- Ann Henderson-Sellers
  Royal Melbourne Institute of Technology, Australia
- John Houghton
  *Co-Chair, Intergovernmental Panel on Climate Change
  Working Group II, UK*
- Phil Jones
  University of East Anglia, UK
- Igor L. Karol
  Main Geophysical Observatory, Russia
- Murari Lal
  Indian Institute of Technology, India
- Jerry D. Mahlman
  National Oceanic and Atmospheric Administration, USA
- Pim Martens
  University of Limburg, The Netherlands
- Mario J. Molina
  Massachusetts Institute of Technology, USA
- Henning Rodhe
  University of Stockholm, Sweden
- Keith P. Shine
  University of Reading, UK
- Peter E.O. Usher
  United Nations Environment Programme, Kenya

**This document answers some of the most commonly asked questions
about the impact of human activity on climate change.**
www.gcrio.org/ipcc/qa/contributors.html

Text 5–2: Common questions about climate change

COMMON QUESTIONS
ABOUT CLIMATE CHANGE

This document answers some of the most commonly asked questions about climate change, including whether the Earth has warmed, which human activities are contributing to climate change, what further climatic changes are expected to occur, and what effects these changes may have on humans and the environment.

5 First, however, several issues have to be clarified: what the Earth's climate is, how climate differs from weather, and what processes influence climate.

Climate is the average weather, including seasonal extremes and variations, either locally, regionally, or across the globe. In any one location, weather can change very rapidly from day to day and from year to year, even within an unchanging climate.

10 These changes involve shifts in, for example, temperatures, precipitation, winds, and clouds. In contrast to weather, climate is generally influenced by slow changes in features like the ocean, the land, the orbit of the Earth about the sun, and the energy output of the sun.

Fundamentally, climate is controlled by the long-term balance of energy of the

15 Earth and its atmosphere. Incoming radiation from the sun, mainly in the form of visible light, is absorbed at the Earth's surface and in the atmosphere above. On average, absorbed radiation is balanced by the amount of energy returned to space in the form of infrared 'heat' radiation. Greenhouse gases such as water vapour and carbon dioxide, as well as clouds and small particles (called 'aerosols'), trap some

20 heat in the lower part of the Earth's atmosphere. This is called the greenhouse effect. If there was no natural greenhouse effect, the average surface temperature would be about 34°C (61°F) colder than it is today.

Winds and ocean currents redistribute heat over the surface of the Earth. The evaporation of surface water and its subsequent condensation and precipitation in

25 the atmosphere redistribute heat between the Earth's surface and the atmosphere, and between different parts of the atmosphere.

Natural events cause changes in climate. For example, large volcanic eruptions put tiny particles in the atmosphere that block sunlight, resulting in a surface cooling of a few years' duration. Variations in ocean currents change distribution of heat and

30 precipitation. El Niño events (periodic warming of the central and eastern tropical Pacific Ocean) typically last one to two years and change weather patterns around the world, causing heavy rains in some places and droughts in others. Over longer time spans, tens or hundreds of thousands of years, natural changes in the geographical distribution of energy received from the sun and the amounts of greenhouse gases and

35 dust in the atmosphere have caused the climate to shift from ice ages to relatively warmer periods, such as the one we are currently experiencing.

Human activities can also change the climate. The atmospheric amounts of many greenhouse gases are increasing, especially that of carbon dioxide, which has increased by 30% over the last 200 years, primarily as a result of changes in land use

40 (e.g. deforestation) and of burning coal, oil, and natural gas (e.g. in automobiles, industry, and electricity generation). If current trends in emissions were to continue, the amount of carbon dioxide in the atmosphere would double during the twenty-first century,

with further increases thereafter. The amounts of several other greenhouse gases would increase substantially as well.

45   The accumulation of greenhouse gases in the atmosphere due to human activities will change the climate by enhancing the natural greenhouse effect, leading to an increase in the Earth's average surface temperature. This warming may be partially offset in certain regions where air pollution leads to high concentrations of small particles in the atmosphere that block sunlight.

50   The current best estimate of the expected rise of globally averaged surface temperature relative to 1991 is 1 to 3.5°C (about 2 to 6°F) by the year 2100, with continued increases thereafter. Because most greenhouse gases remain in the atmosphere for a long period of time, even if emissions from human activities were to stop immediately, effects of past emissions would persist for centuries.

55   The Intergovernmental Panel on Climate Change (IPCC), cosponsored by the United Nations Environment Programme and the World Meteorological Organization and made up of over 2,000 scientific and technical experts from around the world, published its First Assessment Report in 1990 and its Second Assessment Report in 1996. The Second Report contains over 10,000 references and is over 2,000 pages in
60   length. Although our understanding of some details of climate change is still evolving, the IPCC report is the most comprehensive and scientifically authoritative account of our understanding of climate change, the potential impact on humans and the natural environment, the technology currently available to reduce human influences on climate, and the socio-economic implications of possible measures to mitigate these
65   changes. The document that follows has been written and reviewed by scientists who participated in the IPCC process, and it attempts to answer some of the most commonly asked questions about these issues, based upon information contained in the IPCC reports. A list of the scientists who prepared this document is provided inside the front cover.

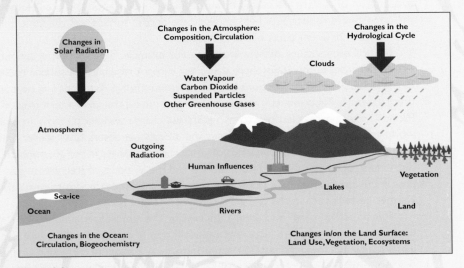

Figure 1.1

Schematic view of components of the global climate system, some of their processes and interactions, and some aspects that can cause climate change.

ARE HUMAN ACTIVITIES
CONTRIBUTING TO CLIMATE CHANGE?

A comprehensive assessment by the IPCC of the scientific evidence suggests that human activities are contributing to climate change, and that there has been a discernible human influence on global climate.

Climate changes caused by human activities, most importantly the burning of
5 fossil fuels (coal, oil, and natural gas) and deforestation, are superimposed on, and to some extent masked by, natural climate fluctuations. Natural changes in climate result from interactions such as those between the atmosphere and ocean, referred to as internal factors, and from external causes, such as variations in the sun's energy output and in the amount of material injected into the upper atmosphere by
10 explosive volcanic eruptions.

Studies that aim to identify human influences on climate attempt to separate a human-caused climate-change factor (the signal) from the background noise of natural climate variability. Such investigations usually consist of two parts: detection of an unusual change, and attribution of all or part of that change to a particular cause or causes.

15 The concepts of detection and attribution may be understood in terms of a simple medical analogy. Measurement of a body temperature of 40°C (104°F) detects the presence of some abnormal condition or symptom, but does not in itself give the cause of the symptom. To attribute the symptom to an underlying cause often requires additional and more complex tests, such as chemical analyses
20 of blood and urine, or even X-rays and CAT scans.

Early work on climate change detection examined changes in the globally averaged surface temperature of the Earth over the last century. Most studies of this type concluded that the observed increase of roughly 0.5°C (about 1°F) was larger than would be expected as a result of natural climate variability alone.

25 Observed globally averaged temperature changes have also been analysed away from the Earth's surface. The observations used come from conventional weather observing instruments (radiosondes) and from satellites. As expected, because of the different factors affecting the variability of and persistence of temperatures at different altitudes, there are noticeable differences between short-term trends at
30 the surface and those at higher altitudes. The record of temperatures away from the Earth's surface, which spans only the past 40 years compared with the much longer surface record, is too short for globally averaged values to provide any definitive information about the extent of human influences.

The further step of attributing some part of observed temperature changes to
35 human influences makes use of climate models, which have been employed to estimate the climatic effects of a range of human-induced and natural factors. The human factors include recent changes in the atmospheric concentrations of both greenhouse gases and sulphate particles (called 'aerosols'). The natural factors include solar variability, the effects of volcanic eruptions, and internal variability of the climate system resulting
40 from interactions among its individual components.

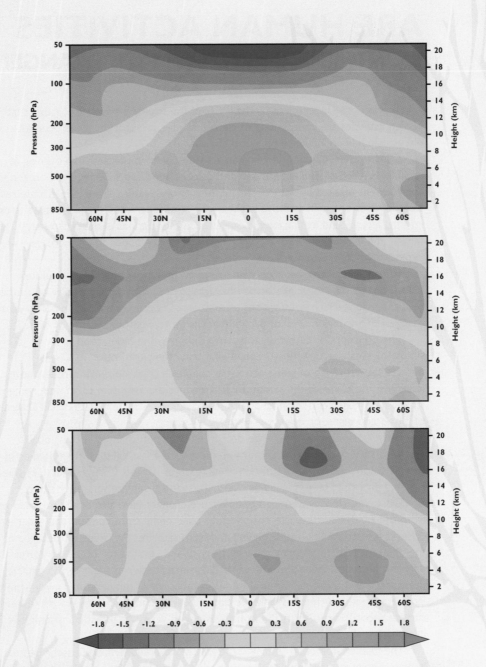

Figure 2.1

Modelled and observed changes in atmospheric temperature, from close to the Earth's surface to the lower stratosphere. Model results are from two sets of experiments: with 'present-day' levels of atmospheric carbon dioxide (panel a), and with present-day carbon dioxide, sulphur emissions, and stratospheric ozone depletion (panel b). They are given as changes relative to a pre-industrial state of the atmosphere. Observed changes (panel c) are temperature trends over the period 1963 to 1988, as estimated from weather balloons. All results are for annually averaged data and are in units of degrees Celsius (panels a, b) and degrees Celsius/25 years (panel c). The patterns of change in panels b and c are similar.

Text 5–3: Are human activities contributing to climate change? cont.

The changes in globally averaged temperature that have occurred at the Earth's surface over the past century are similar in size and timing to those predicted by models that take into account the combined influences of human factors and solar variability.

To probe the question of attribution requires the application of more powerful
45 and complex methods, beyond the use of global averages alone. New studies have focused on comparing maps or patterns of temperature change in observations and in models. Pattern analysis is the climatological equivalent of the more comprehensive tests in the medical analogy mentioned previously, and makes it possible to achieve more definitive attribution of observed climate changes to a
50 particular cause or causes.

The expected influence of human activities is thought to be much more complex than uniform warming over the entire surface of the Earth and over the whole seasonal cycle. Patterns of change over space and time therefore provide a more powerful analysis technique. The basic idea underlying pattern-based approaches is
55 that different potential causes of climate change have different characteristic patterns of climate response or fingerprints. Attribution studies seek to obtain a fingerprint match between the patterns of climate change predicted by models and those actually observed.

Comparisons between observed patterns of temperature change and those
60 predicted by models have now been made at the Earth's surface and in vertical sections through the atmosphere (Figure 2.1). Model predictions show increasing agreement with changes observed over the past 30–50 years. The closest agreement occurs when the combined effects of greenhouse gases and sulphate aerosol particles are considered. Statistical analyses have shown that these correspondences are highly
65 unlikely to have occurred by chance.

The agreements between the patterns of change predicted by models and those actually observed are due to similarities at large spatial scales, such as contrasts between the temperature changes in the northern and southern hemispheres or between different levels of the atmosphere. It is at these large scales that we have
70 most confidence in model performance. More importantly, many of the results of these studies agree with our physical understanding of the climate system, and do not depend solely on numerical models or statistical techniques.

There are still uncertainties in these detection and attribution studies. These are due primarily to our imperfect knowledge of the true climate-change signal
75 due to human activities, to our incomplete understanding of the background noise of natural climatic variability against which this signal must be detected, and to inadequacies in the observational record. Such uncertainties make it difficult to determine the exact size of the human contribution to climate change. Nevertheless, the most recent assessment of the science suggests that human
80 activities have led to a discernible influence on global climate and that these activities will have an increasing influence on future climate.

WHAT HUMAN ACTIVITIES
CONTRIBUTE TO CLIMATE CHANGE

The burning of coal, oil, and natural gas, as well as deforestation and various agricultural and industrial practices, are altering the composition of the atmosphere and contributing to climate change. These human activities have led to increased atmospheric concentrations of a number of greenhouse gases, including carbon
5 dioxide, methane, nitrous oxide, chlorofluorocarbons, and ozone in the lower atmosphere. The importance of these gases is shown in Figure 3.1.

Carbon dioxide is produced when coal, oil, and natural gas (fossil fuels) are burned to produce energy used for transportation, manufacturing, heating, cooling, electricity generation, and other applications (see Figure 3.2). The use of fossil fuel currently
10 accounts for 80 to 85% of the carbon dioxide being added to the atmosphere.

Land use changes, e.g. clearing land for logging, ranching, and agriculture, also lead to carbon dioxide emissions. Vegetation contains carbon that is released as carbon dioxide when the vegetation decays or burns. Normally, lost vegetation would be replaced by regrowth with little or no net emission of carbon dioxide. However,
15 over the past several hundred years, deforestation and other land use changes in many countries have contributed substantially to atmospheric carbon dioxide increases. Although deforestation is still occurring in some parts of the northern hemisphere, on the whole, regrowth of vegetation in the north appears to be taking some carbon dioxide out of the atmosphere. Most of the net carbon dioxide
20 emissions from deforestation are currently occurring in tropical regions. Land use changes are responsible for 15 to 20% of current carbon dioxide emissions.

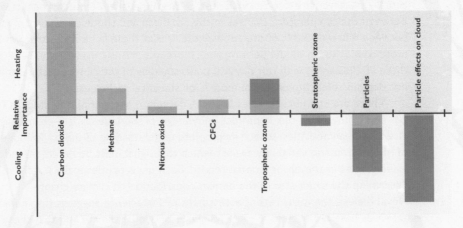

Figure 3.1
Relative importance of the various greenhouse gases and small particles currently in the atmosphere. Bars extending above the horizontal line indicate a warming effect. Bars extending below the horizontal line indicate a cooling effect. The impacts of tropospheric ozone, stratospheric ozone, and particles are quite uncertain. The range of possible effects for these gases is indicated by the bar on the darker shading; i.e., the effect is in the range of one end of the darker shading to the other.

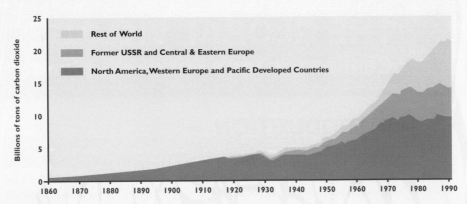

Figure 3.2

Carbon dioxide emissions from the burning of coal, oil, and natural gas are shown for the period 1860 to 1995 for three groups of countries.

Methane (natural gas) is the second most important of the greenhouse gases resulting from human activities. It is produced by rice cultivation, cattle and sheep ranching, and by decaying material in landfills. Methane is emitted during coal mining and
25 oil drilling, and by leaky gas pipelines. Human activities have increased the concentration of methane in the atmosphere by about 145% above what would be present naturally.

Nitrous oxide is produced by various agricultural and industrial practices. Human activities have increased the concentration of nitrous oxide in the atmosphere by about 15% above what would be present naturally.

30 Chlorofluorocarbons (CFCs) have been used in refrigeration, air conditioning, and as solvents. However, the production of these gases is being eliminated under existing international agreements because they deplete the stratospheric ozone layer. Other fluorocarbons that are also greenhouse gases are being used as substitutes for CFCs in some applications, for example in refrigeration and air conditioning. Although currently
35 very small, their contributions to climate change are expected to rise.

Ozone in the troposphere, that is, in the lower part of the atmosphere, is another important greenhouse gas resulting from industrial activities. It is created naturally and also by reactions in the atmosphere involving gases resulting from human activities, including nitrogen oxides from motor vehicles and power plants. Based on current
40 data, tropospheric ozone is an important contributor to the enhanced greenhouse effect. However, in part because ozone is also produced naturally, and because of its relatively short atmospheric lifetime, the magnitude of this contribution is uncertain.

Contrary to popular perception, the Antarctic ozone hole does not cause global warming. Instead, the global depletion of stratospheric ozone caused by CFCs and
45 other gases has resulted in a small cooling effect as shown in Figure 3.1.

Human activities, such as the burning of fossil fuels and changes in land use, have increased the abundance of small particles in the atmosphere. These particles can change the amount of energy that is absorbed and reflected by the atmosphere. They are also believed to modify the properties of clouds, changing the amount of
50 energy that they absorb and reflect. Intensive studies of the climatic effects of these particles began only recently and the overall effect is uncertain. It is likely that the net effect of these small particles is to cool the climate and to partially offset the warming of increasing concentrations of greenhouse gases.

THE GLOBAL VILLAGE:
Challenges for a shrinking planet

INTRODUCTION

Since the Canadian academic Marshall McLuhan coined the phrase 'global village' in 1969, home computers, cable television, satellite-linked mobile phones and the Internet have been added to the array of new technologies drawing the peoples of the world together. But McLuhan also pointed out that the tribal-global village is not 'the place
5 to find ideal peace and harmony'. Village conditions bring into focus the myriad differences between people and cultures.

Multinationals seeking to exploit the potential of economic globalisation are often advised to 'think global, act local'. While the idea of a single global purchasing culture may appeal to big business, the reality is that people's buying habits are determined as
10 much by culture as by income – and cultures vary greatly from place to place. What sells well in Japan may stay on the shelves in Canada. While some products appear to have global appeal, selling methods and local specifications may vary considerably. Even in the European Union, where trading and political ties are especially strong, there are major differences in customer behaviour. Advertising which works for Italians may turn
15 off Scandinavians. The German consumer products market is different from that in neighbouring France. This multiplicity in buying patterns extends to many other aspects of daily life – politics, food, hobbies, education and sexual relations. Even with a single country, diversity is often more apparent than homogeneity. Lager louts who like to create mayhem in the streets of Paris may share a plane home with culture vultures on
20 an art appreciation tour. Every city is a mishmash of humanity of all shades, habits and opinions. On a global scale, this variety is almost infinite.

It is sometimes argued that developments in transport and telecommunications, along with the collapse of communism, have resulted in the 'deaths' of distance, geography and history. In other words, people share the same view of the world whichever continent
25 they inhabit. They are joined together by a desire to enjoy freedom, material comfort, and security. Television and the Internet have created new links between people worldwide. Sport, fashion and entertainment have become global industries. Political cooperation between nations, especially in Europe but also in intergovernmental forums in Latin America, East Asia and Africa, is much greater than it was before World War II. For all its
30 weaknesses, the UN system provides an extraordinary concentration of intergovernmental debate and cooperation. The growth of trade, tourism and foreign investment strengthens the bonds between countries and should make them less likely to fight each other. Conversely, any country which gets left out of the global system or feels threatened by it, may be tempted to lash out. Hence concerns over, for example, North Korea or Iraq.

35 In terms of economic management, the World Bank model (based on western thinking) is used almost everywhere. Yet opinions differ strongly on the effectiveness of 'structural adjustment programmes' and the mix of private/public control over economic activity. The Asian financial crisis may throw up more resistance to the idea of aping the US model of society, flawed by urban deprivation and violent crime. The 'global village' is
40 perhaps closest in the financial world, where London, Tokyo, New York and about 20 other cities dominate a 24-hour global trading system for stocks, bonds, currencies, commodities

and financial derivatives. In this screen-based village, vast sums are transferred back and forth in deals which are mostly speculative rather than directly connected to trade in merchandise or services. This 'virtual' economy can have a huge impact on real lives in
45 every part of the world. The power and global reach of the money men causes unease among both peoples and governments. While poorer countries feel exposed to economic domination by the West, the growing business habit of 'outsourcing' (i.e. exporting jobs) creates new tensions in richer nations, where public concern over the environment has also increased. The World Trade Organisation (WTO) regulates trade but does not address the
50 social or ecological consequences of global business activity – a shortcoming which many feel must be urgently addressed.

The disengagement of the global financial system from the real economy is a worrying development, especially in the light of potential penetration by organised crime. The problem with this and other aspects of globalisation is that there are no
55 effective global authorities to control it. Nations are very reluctant to share sovereignty with other countries, so the move towards effective supranational institutions is slow. The US, which did so much to create the UN system in the 1940s, has become increasingly laggard in this respect. Unfortunately, the global village lacks an effective police force.

THE SHRINKING PLANET

Telecommunications and transportation systems have weakened the barriers of geography which separate different peoples. Yet many cultural differences persist.

Global communications – global understanding?

5 In 1995, according to the International Telecommunication Union (ITU), there were 211 TV sets for every 1,000 people in the world. Even in sub-Saharan Africa there were 43 sets per thousand people. Few cultural groups are so isolated that they
10 don't know how their fellow humans live. But this knowledge can increase discontent as well as cultural convergence. According to *Time* magazine, the 1998 football World Cup accumulated a total TV audience of 37 billion people – more than six times the global population.
15 Brazil's young star Ronaldo became one of the best-known people in the world. Similar fame has been accorded to media 'stars' as diverse as President Clinton, Arnold Schwarzenegger and the Pope.

For most of human history, the picture of the world which most people had was determined by their immediate surroundings. There was no way of knowing what was
20 happening on the other side of the planet – other than from the stories and artefacts brought back by a few sailors, explorers or merchants.

The 20th century has seen a profound change. Not only has the population exploded (from 2 billion in 1930 to about 6 billion now), but technology has enabled tribesmen in Central Africa or Borneo to watch TV programmes about life in New

25 York or Paris; throngs of tourists visit the most remote corners of the globe, bringing with them new ideas, customs and languages; aboriginal groups have learned to use the Internet to publicise their grievances at the encroachment of alien modern cultures which threaten tribal traditions; books written in Germany or Canada are routinely printed in Spain or Hong Kong; components of motor cars designed in Japan may

30 be made in a dozen different countries before being assembled in Mexico or Poland; people in Korea or Tanzania may share admiration for Manchester United, Michael Jackson, Ronaldo or Princess Diana; wearing jeans, eating burgers and listening to rock music have become the daily habit of youngsters across the globe.

Yet such apparently universal links may be more superficial than they seem. An Iranian

35 youth cannot easily shake off the Islamic culture in which he grew up. While Shanghai teenagers may appear to have more in common with their counterparts in Los Angeles than with the older generation in other oriental cities, they remain distinctly Chinese, affected by their national culture, history and language. Just as it is possible for an individual to be a 'good European' as well as a proud Scotsman, so fellow citizens of the 'global village' can

40 share many tastes and yet be as different from each other as chalk from cheese.

Sharing common interests and buying similar products do not obliterate human peculiarities. Indeed, the homogenising effect of globalisation is partly offset by computer technology which allows for easy customisation of products. A 'world car' may have the same 'platform', but is sold with different shapes, colours and accessories to meet local

45 requirements. Ownership of global media is highly concentrated, but communication is being fragmented as digital technology enables hundreds of TV channels to be beamed to different audiences with their own viewing tastes and receiving languages.

ECONOMIC GLOBALISATION

Money is increasingly stateless, with most countries abandoning exchange controls. Businesses of all sizes can now operate on a global basis.

The global marketplace

Money and goods are moved from country to country

5 with little regard for distances or borders. More and more services are traded internationally. On the other hand, labour remains largely immobile (and therefore vulnerable to job losses) – an anomaly which can have serious social implications. The growth in international

10 trade is a telling indicator of the globalisation of business in recent decades. Between 1900 and 1950, world trade barely doubled. Since then, the volume of trade has risen twelvefold. In OECD countries, the majority of goods used by households and industries

15 include imported materials or parts. Complex manufacturing activities now span the globe.

A Perhaps the most obvious sign of globalisation is in the economic area. The logos of corporate giants such as Coca-Cola, Nike, Shell and Mercedes are a common sight in cities on every continent. While trade has long been a part of the international scene, its

20 volume has rocketed in the last decade, along with foreign capital investment. Business operates in a worldwide environment, with competition in faraway countries as much of a threat to a manufacturer or service provider as a rival in a neighbouring town.

B In 1996, foreign direct investment (FDI) around the world was $553 billion – more than twice the figure for 1990 ($239 billion). The biggest recipient countries were the US

25 ($77 billion), China ($40 billion), the UK ($32 billion) and France ($22 billion), followed by Brazil ($10 billion), Singapore ($9 billion), Indonesia, the Netherlands and Mexico ($8 billion each), and Australia, Canada and Spain ($6 billion each). Some $15 billion was invested in the former Soviet bloc in Europe and Central Asia. Elsewhere in the developing world, Malaysia, Peru, India, Argentina, Chile, Colombia, Thailand, Venezuela,

30 Vietnam, the Philippines and Nigeria all had FDI exceeding $1 billion. Meanwhile, global merchandise exports grew from $1.9 trillion in 1980 to $5.4 trillion in 1996. Trade in services has leapt ahead too. For example, it has become commonplace for European airlines to get their computer programming done in Asia and for banks, accountants and advertising agencies to sell their services in dozens of different countries.

C Services and intellectual property rights are now covered by the international rules of the World Trade Organisation, making it easier and more lucrative for companies to sell services and know-how across borders. Trade in goods has been encouraged by the fall in tariff barriers brought about by successive GATT[1] rounds. The weighted mean tariff for products entering the European Union was down to 5% by 1997 and just

40 over 4% in the US. The comparative figure for Japan was less than 3%. India's weighted mean tariff fell from 83% in 1990 to 27.7% in 1997 as it gradually opened itself to international trade and investment.

D Of course, tariffs do not tell the whole story, since trade can equally be impeded by cultural differences, domestic regulation, language barriers and, as the World Bank

45 delicately puts it, 'private collusive behaviour and information asymmetries'.

E The three most powerful trading blocs are the EU, APEC and NAFTA, which together account for over 90% of international trade. Economic globalisation is a phenomenon which impacts on all countries but which is of main benefit to the industrialised world – which has goods to sell and money to buy. Africa, the 'lost

50 continent', has increased its trade with the outside world but its share of global FDI and trade is tiny.

F One of the dangers of economic globalisation is the further concentration of power in those who are already rich. The gap between rich and poor nations has widened in recent years, despite the catch-up success of a few countries such as the Asian 'tigers'.

55 A similar division is taking place between individual haves and have-nots even within the industrialised countries. Those without money are pushed to the margins of society, while commercial thinking spreads from business to penetrate socio-cultural sectors such as education, health care, the arts and even religion.

G Globalisation, as driven largely by short-term economic pressures, is based on

60 consumerism, with people being regarded primarily as 'customers'. They are segmented by income group rather than by cultural differences. The value of, say, social manners or communal worship tends to be submerged, along with 'non-economic' considerations such as animal rights or the 'health' of the oceans.

1 After 1947, rules for international trade were negotiated by member states in the General Agreement on Tariffs and Trade (GATT) – the US congress having rejected the idea of an international trade organisation as part of the original UN system. For over 40 years, the GATT remained a provisional set of international trading rules rather than a regulatory authority as such. The last round of GATT negotiations, known as the Uruguay Round, was completed in 1994. It greatly extended the range of trade covered and finally established the World Trade Organisation, based in Geneva, to act as a global regulatory authority.

H   Yet the image of global business as a juggernaut destroying everything in its path is
65 misleading. Companies may try to shape consumer demand but cannot disregard
customer concerns such as health and environment. The more sophisticated companies
take care to emphasise their social responsibilities, working more closely with
governments and NGOs to ensure that 'sustainability' is built into their long-term
business plans. For example, Unilever's support for the Marine Stewardship Council
70 shows how economic power can be used to protect global resources.

Competition and protection

The pressures of global competition may tempt some countries to protect their own
workers from job losses by increasing trade barriers. Advocates of free trade argue
that such policies result in a vicious circle of retaliatory action – and point to the
75 protectionist, war-provoking 1930s as a grim example.

*The increase in global trade means that exchange
rate fluctuations now play a major role in determining
business success or failure. Even the best-managed
company can be destroyed by a sudden move in the
80 exchange rates. For example, businesses in Japan
had to contend with a fall in the exchange rate of the
yen from 111 to the US dollar in mid-1970 to 147 in
August 1998. During the same period, the Indonesian
rupiah fell from 2,500 to 14,000.*

85 The supermarket has replaced the corner shop as
the symbol of household consumerism in the global
village. In the West, the contents of a typical house
contain products from every corner of the globe.
Supermarket shelves are stacked with food brought
90 from dozens of countries. In a pre-industrial village,
what was available was largely determined by what
could be grown on surrounding farms. No such
limitations exist in the global village.

Global financial markets

95 Financial services in the global village are heavily concentrated in a few OECD
countries. For example, the world's stock markets carried a market capitalisation
value of $20,178 billion in 1997, with the US accounting for 42% of this vast sum. The
leading stock markets (measured by the capital value of all stocks listed in 1997) were:

	$ billion
US	8,484
Japan	3,089
UK	1,740
Germany	671
China (inc. HK)	656
France	591

100

105

Note that US stock market
capitalisation grew from $3,059 billion
in 1990, while Japan's total barely
increased from its 1990 level. Market
capitalisation of the Hong Kong
exchange rose from $83 billion in 1990
to $450 billion in 1996, China's from $2
billion to $206 billion.

In mid-1998, the Frankfurt and London stock exchanges announced that they planned to
develop a joint electronic trading platform. Other European exchanges may decide to join
later, raising the prospect of a single European stock exchange – though Paris initially
110 reacted to the Anglo-German plan by proposing its own combination of exchanges.

Global financial markets - continued

The large OECD countries dominate global banking, and trade in foreign exchange, commodity futures, stocks and shares, and financial 'derivatives'. Global derivatives contracts were valued at $55.5 trillion in 1995. The combined weight of these money
115 markets, whose activity (including daily turnover of $1.2 trillion in foreign exchange) is largely speculative – as opposed to being driven by merchandise trade ($5 trillion a year) – dwarfs global GNP ($27.8 trillion). This situation has led some commentators to describe the global financial system as 'casino capitalism' which has spun out of control and threatens the 'real economy'. Electronic funds transfers have greatly increased the
120 difficulty of controlling (and taxing) flows of money from country to country.

Whereas the World Trade Organisation provides a global regulatory body for international trade in goods and services, there is no equivalent body for the regulation of global money markets.

COMMUNITY & CONFLICT

Citizens of the global village tend to be the better educated and more prosperous of the world's people. It is a new minority group, surrounded by the poor.

A There is no inherent conflict between being a good global citizen and being a proud
5 member of a particular regional or ethnic group, nation state or city. The same person may regard himself as a 'European' or an 'African' while endorsing the universal brotherhood of man. Such multi-layering of identities is common. Humans long to be part of a group, while insisting on their individuality. The habit of treating a different tribe as the enemy may be accompanied by great hospitality towards strangers. Awareness of the planet's
10 fragility may have brought moves towards the globalisation of human society, but the propensity to violent conflict seems as well-honed as ever. If global war now seems unlikely, civil wars still rage worldwide.

Global village – global inequality

There is little sign that the economic benefits of the global village will be evenly
15 distributed. The income gap between rich and poor has widened over the last 50 years. The technology gap has yawned wider still.

B Ethnic divisions have not vanished but may gradually diminish under the influence of globalisation. Coke and Pepsi show their customers as smiling multi-ethnic crowds, implying that the world is already united in its love of soft drinks. Teenagers have their own global
20 culture based on fashion, pop music, sports heroes and clothes. Sport is both unifying and polarising in its effect, with supporters cheering their own team and jeering their opponents.
C More and more countries are becoming multi-ethnic, embracing large numbers of foreigners. Though this creates tensions at first, the longer-term trend appears to be greater acceptance of multi-cultural society. Urbanisation, another global phenomenon,
25 has accelerated this trend, for it is easier to introduce new cultures in the relative

anonymity of the city than it is in tradition-bound rural villages. In OECD countries almost 80% of the population live in towns – compared to 31% in China and 27% in India. In global terms, the majority of people (54%) still live in rural areas. Yet rapid urbanisation is a common feature of almost every developing country. New ideas and
30 fashions – and diseases – spread fast in cities. In major urban centres of even the poorest countries there is a core of privileged people with access to computers, mobile phones, electric razors, imported wines and other trappings of the global village.

D   A century ago agriculture employed over half the workforce even in rapidly industrialising countries. Today the global average is still over 45%. But in the UK and
35 USA, farm workers now make up less than 3% of the workforce. Some experts have suggested that a similar contraction is happening in manufacturing, as technology enables more products to be made by computer-controlled machines. Services already account for 70% of employment in the USA. Since agriculture and manufacturing have provided the bulk of employment for hundreds of years, the transition to a radically different pattern of
40 employment is bound to be difficult. Blaming the loss of jobs on globalisation is a typical reaction, with foreigners bearing the brunt of labour force discontent.

E   In 1995, Germany's population included over 7 million foreigners (compared with the UK's 2 million). Germany received 788,000 immigrants in 1995. In Australia, foreign-born workers make up 24% of the total labour force. The US has about 25 million foreign-born
45 residents, accounting for about 9% of the workforce. There was a legal inflow of 721,000 in 1995 (compared with 1.5 million in 1990). Illegal immigrants probably number at least a million a year. Foreigners make up 19% of the Swiss population and 9% of the population in Austria and Belgium. The Middle East is home to large numbers of immigrant workers from Egypt, Pakistan, Bangladesh and the Philippines. Workers from Bolivia and Paraguay
50 go to Argentina in search of a better life, just as Turks go to Germany, Mexicans to the US and Algerians to France.

F   Whether the world is more prone to conflict than it used to be is hard to say. Perhaps we are just more aware of violent confrontation in different parts of the world. A famine in remote Sudan gets media coverage whereas a century ago starving populations might
55 die unseen. Today's wars can be watched live on television, like Hollywood action movies. Greater awareness of the human consequences of battle may reduce the lust for war – or make it another spectator sport.

Fringe groups everywhere

The proliferation of nationalist militia groups in the
60 US – there are over 400 groups with paramilitary training sites in over 20 states – is but one sign of the fragmentation of modern society. Hundreds of other fringe groups and 'eccentric' individuals have been strengthened by the ability to link with others
65 through television and over the Internet. Thus behaviour which was once regarded as bizarre or anti-social, is increasingly regarded as a 'normal' part of the multi-cultural society.

G   Computer-mediated communication (CMC) is being used in more and more
70 countries as a way to enhance democracy. Over 200 cities worldwide have civic networking projects experimenting in information access and citizens' feedback and even voting. However, CMC is also used by less desirable groups such as paedophile

75 rings, gun salesmen, pornographers and political extremists. For example, the Thule-Netz in Germany provides an Internet-based information exchange which has different levels of access – to ensure that only genuine right-wing activists know what is being planned. Use of the World Wide Web gets round the problem of Germany's domestic ban on the distribution of Nazi propaganda.

H This example highlights a more general problem – how to enforce national law in the global village. Laws enacted to protect the people and environment of one country
80 are increasingly undermined by new 'global' technology (e.g. electronic funds transfer) or by international agreements (e.g. greenhouse gas emissions) which tend to use a 'lowest common denominator' approach in order to get consent from as many nations as possible. Organised crime has been particularly adept at exploiting the weaknesses in global law enforcement, growing at a much faster rate than most legitimate businesses.
85 Organised crime is a major beneficiary of the global village.

Cultural diversity

Cultural diversity is one of the glories of human civilisation. For example, Chiapas Indians, using caricature blond wigs and pale-faced masks, adapted Spanish cultural imports to their own use after the invasion by Cortes in the 16th century. Similarly,
90 Western cultural exports of the late 20th century (and early 21st century) are being adapted in different ways in different parts of the world. Gunpowder and disease overthrew native societies in the colonial era. Television, mobile phones and soft drinks may do the same for traditional societies in the 21st century. A major complaint of today's Chiapas-based Zapatistas movement in Mexico is the damage done to
95 native cultures by global capitalism and the exclusion of the masses from the benefits which globalisation is supposed to bring.

THE SHARING OF SOVEREIGNTY

There is more and more cooperation – and even pooled sovereignty – between states. Every country is strongly influenced by external factors beyond its control.

It is sometimes argued that globalisation is breaking down the system of nation states
5 upon which international relations has largely depended. Just as families once combined into tribes and tribes into nations, so nations are combining into regional power blocs, and thence perhaps to a single world political community. Such an outcome is a very long way off, but there is certainly far more cooperation between nations than there was 50 years ago. Indeed, there is now a vast network of international organisations, at
10 both government and non-government levels, bringing people together to work on the practical issues of living together in harmony.

While nation states remain the chief building blocks of the global system, they are by no means the only players on the scene. Chief among international organisations is the United Nations – much maligned for its inability to solve the world's most intractable
15 problems (civil war, poverty, etc.) yet an essential tool for the prevention of global anarchy. In fact, the UN has provided an invaluable forum for the exchange of views and has provided the main coordinating centre to deal with mundane but vital rules to ensure that

international mail gets delivered, that aircraft can fly across borders in safety, that food and industrial goods meet specified health and safety standards. These daily achievements of
20 UN agencies go unreported, while failures of peace-making get much media attention.

Bearing in mind the pressures on competing nations, it is perhaps surprising that any major decisions can be made on a joint basis. That the European Union was able to agree (in 1986) on a majority voting system to advance the single market was an extraordinary development in international relations. The EU has gone even further
25 along this path with the agreement by 11 of its 15 member states to pursue economic and monetary union, including the use of a single currency. In the EU, at least, national sovereignty over economic matters has been pooled among 11 governments.

Other bodies which tie Europe's nations closer together include the European Free Trade Association, the Western European Union, the Council of Europe and the
30 Organisation for Security and Cooperation in Europe. NATO provides a military alliance which links the US and Canada with Europe, and talks in the top-level 'Transatlantic Business Dialogue' envisage a free trade area embracing both the European Union and North America.

Even the superpower US has relinquished some of its sovereignty by, for example,
35 joining the World Trade Organisation and agreeing to abide by its rules. It will be interesting to see how often the WTO's dispute settlement procedures are called into play over the next decade and whether major economic powers can be made to toe the line, even when it hurts their domestic business interests. American support is vital if multinational institutions are to work. Yet the US opposed the 1997 Ottawa treaty on landmines and the mid-1998
40 UN decision to establish an International Criminal Court. Getting out of step with global opinion will damage US security options in the long run.

The United Nations

The United Nations organisation provides the nearest thing to a world
45 government. Though its impact is minimal in resolving serious political conflicts, the UN has many valuable functions in smoothing international relations.

The UN is a kind of diplomatic
50 global village, which brings together thousands of government officials from 185 member countries. Their primary aim is the preservation of world peace – though UN work
55 extends to many other objectives. The UN General Assembly, comprising delegates from all UN member states, is more representative of the world community than the 15-nation Security
60 Council, but has far less power. General Assembly resolutions, even when passed with overwhelming majorities, do not bind the Security Council, which is dominated by the
65 'permanent five' – the US, China, Russia, France and the UK.

International law

70 Most law is based on national legislation, but there is a steady accretion of international law. The UN has secured over 300 international treaties since 1945. Most countries have agreed to overriding global laws dealing with such matters as offshore territorial rights, marine pollution, international trade and nuclear proliferation. EU directives take precedence over the national laws of 15 European countries.

Shared sovereignty

75

80

The European Union provides the world's most prominent example of shared sovereignty. Since 1957, the EU has been engaged in an ambitious programme for 'ever closer union among the peoples of Europe'. Eleven of the 15 member states have agreed to a common economic and monetary policy, including the use of a single currency, the euro. Though efforts to develop a common approach to foreign policy have so far failed, most of Western Europe has become a closely integrated economic area, with strong political ties. The Social Chapter lays down broad principles for employee rights, while the EU has led the world in many areas of environmental law. The world's two other main trading blocs, NAFTA and APEC, are not remotely like the EU in terms of political integration and have few of the EU's supranational rules on social and environmental protection.

CONVERGING OR DIVERGING?

Tourism, transport and telecommunications have brought the world closer together, but new cultures are being created as fast as the old ones disappear.

Since 1945 there has been an underlying assumption that the world's poorer countries
5 are gradually 'developing' towards the western model and that international aid policy should be geared to this end. The success of some Asian countries, notably Japan (which was restructured under US guidance after 1945), lent weight to this thesis. Though the World Bank now divides countries into high, middle and low income countries, rather than developed and developing countries, the basic premise has remained – countries
10 afflicted with high levels of poverty, disease and deprivation can improve their standards by adopting western-style institutions and economic management.

The governing elites of almost all states have come to accept that free markets, combined with strict monetary discipline, offer the best path to improving living standards. Country after country has adopted a World Bank-driven 'structural adjustment programme'
15 in an effort to achieve economic success. The orthodox view is that public ownership and protected markets are less efficient than private ownership and free trade. Governments around the globe, encouraged by the World Bank, have been busy privatising state-owned companies in everything from electricity generation and telecommunications to railways and even prisons. The notion of 'public service', whether in health care or broadcasting,
20 has given way to 'private enterprise'.

Average living standards, life expectancy and educational norms have risen strongly in dozens of countries since 1945, though the gap between rich and poor countries is wider than ever. Very few 'developing' states have managed to catch up on the wealthy 'establishment' in North America and Western Europe. Most of the exceptions are in
25 Asia, recently subject to financial meltdown. 'Development' has gone into reverse in Indonesia, and even Japan and South Korea are suffering hardship. In other parts of the world, catching up has been more dream than reality, at least for the vast bulk of the population. Latin America, notorious for its uneven distribution of wealth, has had buoyant stock markets, along with mass poverty. Living conditions in the former Soviet
30 Union have deteriorated for the majority while a few get very rich. Africa has scarcely begun to improve the economic lot of its black population. If there is any global pattern to all this, it seems to be that elites everywhere are doing very well, while 'ordinary people' are facing insecurity and hardship – hardly a major departure from historical precedent. Many people, in both the industrialised and developing worlds, feel that
35 globalisation threatens their jobs, indeed their whole way of life.

There seems to be no way to insulate a modern economy from the forces of global capitalism, yet unease about the direction such forces are taking humanity is by no means confined to Muslims worried about western 'moral corruption', or Buddhists forsaking the material world. Islamist Iran has tried to resist foreign influence, but the
40 weakness of its economy has persuaded it to adopt a more open attitude. In recent years India has also turned away from self-sufficiency to more integration with the world economy. Even North Korea, facing severe food shortages and economic decline, is keen to attract foreign investment.

Tourism has made the retention of traditional cultures more difficult while giving it
45 new economic value – thus local festivals and tribal dances are mounted not as part of regional tradition but as a show for foreign visitors. The Czech Republic (population 10 million) had 17 million tourists in 1996. Most went to Prague, transforming that city from the quiet shabbiness of the communist era to the bustling 'fast-food' commercialism of today. Such developments appear to reinforce the view that the world is being reshaped
50 according to American values.

Of course, tourism is not just an American phenomenon. Germans, Britons, Japanese, Malaysians and many other nationalities travel abroad in very large numbers. The total of overseas tourist visits was close to 600 million in 1996. Cheap air travel has made mass tourism possible, even to the most exotic places. The influx of tourists with different
55 cultural values creates tensions in the receiving community – which may be suppressed when the economic benefit is sufficiently large but may rankle beneath the surface. Yet the local youths who treat foreign visitors with a mixture of envy and contempt may well enjoy listening to rock music and smoking Marlborough cigarettes. They may dream of driving a BMW and having a mobile phone. Their families probably have a Japanese
60 television set. In terms of 'brand allegiance', some global convergence has already taken place. Coca-Cola is an obvious example.

Global broadcasting has even greater impact on popular culture, as was shown by the extraordinary worldwide attention given to the death of Princess Diana (overshadowing the death of Mother Theresa). Watching global news coverage, TV
65 soaps and sporting events is an experience shared by billions. Yet the advent of multi-channel broadcasting will enable viewers to customise their viewing habits. In short, two trends are discernible – a global convergence of certain consumption patterns, combined with a vigorous interest in localised cultures – old and new. Diversity is still the main attribute of the global village.

Text 6–6: Converging or diverging? cont.

The excluded society

70 Poverty and ignorance rule out full participation in the global high-tech economy for much of the world's population. Their exclusion could be a
75 source of growing instability.

'Excluded' from the global consumer society by poverty, Peruvian children know as little about 'information technology' as they do about how their Inca ancestors
80 were able, without the use of machinery, to build walls from massive but perfectly-fitted stone blocks. Power over information and invention has always been confined to elites. Ownership of modern technology is heavily
85 concentrated in a few OECD countries. Yet computers have given ordinary citizens access to more information about technology and government than has ever been available before. Optimists argue that
90 the result will be better education, more opportunity and stronger democracy.

Cultural invasions

Tourist visits worldwide more than doubled between 1980 and 1996,
95 reaching almost 600 million. Television and branded products reach almost every part of the globe. But the way that local populations react to such 'cultural invasions' varies greatly.
100 Networked computers dramatically increase the power of information exchange worldwide – for scientific purposes (accelerating invention), for social and political
105 activism (gathering like-minded individuals) and for business (identifying and selling into new markets). A key characteristic of the Internet is its chaotic diversity. With
110 the advent of digital television, giving viewers hundreds (possibly thousands) of channels to choose from, 'chaotic diversity' may soon overtake television too – though standardised products are more profitable and media ownership is highly concentrated.

Source: Buckley, R. (ed.), 'The Global Village: Challenges for a Shrinking Planet' *Understanding Global Issues* (July 1998)

THE NEW LINGUISTIC ORDER

Text 7–1: The new linguistic order